The Forgotten Black Confederate Fighting Men at the Battle of Painesville, Virginia, April 5, 1865

Copyright © 2023 Phillip Thomas Tucker

All rights reserved, including the right to reproduce this book, or portions thereof in any form. No part of this text may be reproduced, transmitted, downloaded, decompiled, reverse engineered, or stored, in any form or introduced into any information storage and retrieval system, in any form or by any means, whether electronic or mechanical without the express written permission of the author.

The views expressed in this work are solely those of the author and do not necessarily reflect the views of the publisher, and the publisher hereby disclaims any responsibility for them.

Cover images:
Bottom: *The Fall of Richmond, Va on the Night of April 2d 1865,* **Currier & Ives**
Top: **Black Confederate Soldiers**
Shutterstock

ISBN: 9798859652921

PublishNation LLC
www.publishnation.net

Also by this author

Nat Turner's Holy War To Destroy Slavery
America's Female Buffalo Soldier: Cathy Williams
Miller Cornfield at Antietam
Pickett's Charge
Death at the Little Bighorn
Barksdale's Charge
Storming Little Round Top
Exodus From The Alamo
Emily D. West and the "Yellow Rose of Texas" Myth
The South's Finest
George Washington's Surprise Attack
How The Irish Won The American Revolution
Why Custer Was Never Warned
The Alamo's Forgotten Defenders
Ranger Raid
Kings Mountain
History of the Irish Brigade
Custer at Gettysburg
The Alamo's Forgotten Defenders
Miller Cornfield at Antietam
America's Hill of Destiny
The Irish in the American Revolution
Irish Confederates
God Help The Irish!
Burnside's Bridge
The Final Fury
Westerners In Gray
Alexander Hamilton's Revolution
The Confederacy's Fighting Chaplain
Cubans In The Confederacy
Forgotten Stonewall of the West
From Auction Block To Glory
The Important Role of the Irish in the American Revolution
The 1862 Plot to Kidnap Jefferson Davis.
Anne Bonny: The Infamous Female Pirate
America's Forgotten First War for Slavery and Genesis of The Alamo
For Honor, Country, and God: Los Niños Héroes
Targeting Abraham: The Forgotten 1865 Plot To Assassinate Lincoln
A New Look at the Buffalo Soldier Experience in Wartime Vol I: Corporal David Fagen's Metamorphosis and Odyssey
Nanny's War to Destroy Slavery
The Irish at Gettysburg
Blacks in Gray Uniforms
Glory At Fort Wagner: The 54th Massachusetts Vols I, II, and III
Martyred Lieutenant Sanité Bélair

Gran Toya: Founding Mother of Haiti
Claudette Colvin: Forgotten Mother of the Civil Rights Movement
Mulan and the Modern Controversy
Custer's Forgotten Black Soulmate
*The Secret Sexual Sins of the Founding Fathers
and America: Volumes I and II*
Lakshmi Bai
The Trung Sisters
Solitude of Guadeloupe
Brothers of Liberty
Saving Washington's Army
Alexander Hamilton and the Battle of Yorktown
Biden's Folly and America's Turning Point Moment
Biden's Rapid Fall From Grace
Major Robert Rogers and The Racial Dimensions of His Famous 1759 St. Francis Raid
Major Robert Rogers' Tragic Demise
David Fagen: "That Black Devil" of the Philippine-American War
Mary Edmonia Lewis: The Formative Years of America's First Female Black and Native American Sculptress
Female Apache Warrior and Shaman of Her People: The Remarkable Story of Little Sister Lozen
Feminism's and Abolitionism's First Tragic Victim: Olympe de Gouges
Josephine Baker: The Forgotten St. Louis Years That Profoundly Shaped Her
Brothers in Liberty
Charlotte L. Forten's Broken Heart
Russian Invasion of Ukraine Leads the World Closer to Nuclear War
Who Killed Custer?
Ida B. Wells
The Wrath of Britain's Celtic Queen Boudica and her Rebellion Against Rome
"Our Marian" Anderson
The Stono Rebellion 1739
Captain Alexander Hamilton's Forgotten Contributions to Decisive Victory at Trenton, December 26, 1776
Anne Bonny's Adventures in Jamaica's Waters During Her Last Cruise, Autumn 1720
Anne Bonny Outsmarts the British Legal System in the Courtroom and Saves Herself from Hanging
Anne Bonny's Greatest Exploit
Prince Estabrook
Rommel's Wasted Opportunity to Thwart the D-Day Invasion
The Heroic Revolt of the Trung Sisters
Hitler Orders the Death of Field Marshal Rommel
Anne Bonny's Special Place in History and the Meaning of Courage
Hitler's Ignored Orders That Thwarted His Plan to Stop D-Day Invasion
The Greatest Ambush in History
Demise of the Florida Dream

The Forgotten Black Confederate Fighting Men at the Battle of Painesville, Virginia, April 5, 1865

Phillip Thomas Tucker, Ph.D.

Phillip Thomas Tucker, Ph.D. has won recognition as the "Stephen King of History"

Contents

Introduction: The New Historical Myth Making
in the Age of Political Correctness   1

Chapter I: Forgotten Black Valor
From America's Beginning   47

Chapter II: The Richmond Government
Finally Awakens   60

Chapter III: The Forgotten Battle of Painesville,
Virginia, April 5, 1865   73

Epilogue   96

Bibliography   101

About the Author   104

Introduction

The New Historical Myth Making in the Age of Political Correctness

As almost everyone knows, America has been in the process of radically changing on multiple levels in the twenty-first century, especially in cultural terms. The society and culture of the United States have been undergoing extensive transformations in the past few years because of the increasingly dominant political policies and agendas of the political Left during this so-called culture wars, which has been ongoing for decades. These developments have thoroughly politicized practically every aspect of life in the United States in recent years, spilling over into every possible segment of American society today, including even the rewriting of the nation's history. Even now, America's story has been in the process of changing and reshaping by a distinct Left-leaning agenda, which has distorted fundamental historical truths and perpetuated myths at the overall expense of the most fundamental truths and realities about America's story to an alarming degree, even to the point of basically creating historical fiction from a politicized perspective.

Unfortunately, this rather bizarre development that has been changing America and its rich history has been a product of our times and part of the ongoing culture wars between the political Left and Right, which has politicized American life to a degree unimaginable by Americans only a few years before. But the political Left has continued to enjoy the supreme advantage in this cultural struggle over the heart and soul of America because it has controlled the media, school systems, including Ivy League Colleges, and even leading publishing houses, especially university presses that should know better and should have higher standards beyond those of politicization, in America to promote its distorted and anti-historical political agendas at the expense of America's historical truths based on undeniable facts and basic realities.

Today's most blatant and infamous example of the rewriting of American history from the popular Left perspective based on the concept of political correctness has been Nikole Hannah-Jones' much-debated book entitled *The 1619 Project: A New Origin Story*. The extremely weak and flimsy historical thesis at best of this popular book has been the premise that America's true founding resulted when a slave ship sailed into the small port of Jamestown, Virginia, located on the northeastern bank of the muddy James River, on a hot August day in 1619 and brought the first slaves to America. Jamestown of the Virginia Colony, established by the Virginia Company of London, became the first permanent English settlement in America. The colony had been settled by enterprising

Englishmen in 1607 and they had narrowly survived the early years of settlement with considerable difficulty, including from the ravages of starvation when crops failed.

The 1619 Project has been widely proclaimed by today's media and its author as a new origin story for America. However, this new origin story, which is certainly more of a story than history, has embraced by the liberal tenets of the political Left, which has mocked the true founding of America on the nobliest traditions that were primarily based on the Protestant dissenter religion and deep spiritual roots of establishing a New Canaan like the ancient Israelites, because the early settlers from England devoutly followed the dictates and commandants of the Holy Bible. Of course, these settlers included the Pilgrims who settled the Plymouth Colony in Massachusetts in 1620 and then the Puritans of Boston, Massachusetts in 1630. And this religious and spiritual rejuvenation in the New World was especially the case of Reverend John Winthrop's founding of Boston and his famous 1630 "City on a Hill" sermon that promised prosperity and success, if the Puritans, as they were called because they had broken off from the strict and ritualistic Anglican Church of England to find the purest form of worshipping God, lived pure Christian lives, according to God's words and commandments from the Holy Bible.

Predictably, the core tenets of *The 1619 Project* were enthusiastically promoted in the *New York Times,* which is one of the most liberal newspapers in America known for distorting the truth. Even more, this ahistorical book even became a *New York Times* best seller, which hastened its acceptance and entry into American school systems, which have embraced liberalism decades ago, to indoctrinate young minds into the political dictates of the Left's agenda. By this means and across America, historical fiction has been fostered on formative minds who don't know any better and believe the words of their too often Left-leaning teachers, who they usually idolize like generations of youths before them: an effective means of spinning and propagandizing the slanted political views and agendas of the Left and corrupting basic historical truths about America, because the main thesis of *The 1619 Project* is simply not supported by the historical facts and truths. But of course this undeniable historical reality makes no difference to the political Left, because promoting their anti-American agendas has been more important than anything else. Again, this unfortunate situation has been a product and development of these highly politicized times because this much-touted book about an alleged new origin story for America has certainly reflected as much. This controversial work, *The 1619 Project,* was first released in the pages of the *New York Times Magazine* in August 2019. Significantly, this book was not in an academic publication or by a university press, which has revealed a great deal about its substance and quality. Most revealing of all, leading American historians have routinely and thoroughly dismissed *The 1619 Project* as pretty much of a joke today in terms of serious history and for ample good reasons.

An unfortunate trend has developed in the United States of what is little more than the creation of fiction passing as legitimate and serious history in America for largely political reasons during this period of the excessive politicization of America. A new Civil War book was released in 2019, which significantly and symbolically appeared during the same year as when *The 1619 Project* was first published in the *New York Times Magazine* and only two years before the release of *The 1619 Project* in book form. Faithfully following the popular liberal trend like *The 1619 Project*, this new book was released with an outlandish title when it comes to fundamental truths and realities in history, *Searching for Black Confederates, The Civil War's Most Persistent Myth*. The new book was penned by an amateur New England historian, who has long relied on the internet blogs and speaking platforms to get his one-sided messages, historical views, and politicized agendas out to the public almost more like a popular stage performer and actor than a historian, Kevin M. Levin. This new work penned by Levin is comparable to that of the recent book by Nikole Hannah-Jones, incorporating some of the same trademarks of today's popular Left-leaning agendas and tenets that have become trendy and fashionable. These two works are not unlike today's excessive white guilt books, which have become popular in America's politicized environment and with large national presses, from the pens of the descendants of Southern slaveowners, who pour forth their white guilt about slavery on one page after another in what amount to demeaning and embarrassing personal confessions of the "sins of their fathers," although these writers of course had nothing at all to do with slavery in any way, shape, or form.

In a striking but most revealing paradox, Levin decided to write a book to refute what he boldly declared has been the Civil War's most enduring myth, which was actually no myth at all but a historical truth well documented by the historical facts that are quite plentiful, by rather audaciously creating his own myth—a classic case of chutzpah--much like in the case of *The 1619 Project*. Such shameless "historical" endeavors have fully revealed the extent of today's popular trend of rewriting of America's history to fit a political point-of-view that has been extremely slanted and one-sided. This popular myth-creating of American history today has been committed by self-serving and politically driven authors, who have conveniently placed historical facts and truths on the backburner. Levin's 2019 book is but one recent example of the unfortunate process of denying the undeniable facts and realities of history, despite the abundance of the historical facts and documentation that have long proved that large numbers of Black Confederates fought in the South's defense from 1861-1865 and on both sides of the Mississippi River. Nevertheless, the Levin book was written almost as if historical facts and truths no longer make any difference whatsoever, because they seemed not to have mattered to this New England author, who pursued his own agenda and conclusions.

But fundamental historical facts and truths can be neither denied or overturned by recent "history" book based on political agendas and the day's popular and fashionable trends in American society as part of the cultural wars. Even the great Black abolitionist and son of a white master and black slave mother, Frederick Douglass who had escaped Maryland slavery on the Eastern Shore on September 3, 1838, early implored President Abraham Lincoln to enlist black soldiers precisely because the Confederacy was early doing so to augment its ranks in battling against the Union, which he knew from the facts as he had personally discovered. As early as September 1861 and less than six months after Confederate cannon had opened fire on Fort Sumter in Charleston Harbor in mid-April to begin the Civil War, Douglass emphasized in no uncertain terms how: "it is pretty well established, that there are at the present moment many colored men in the Confederate army, doing duty . . . as real soldiers" in the ranks. Even more, the combat roles of Black fighting men in gray uniforms have appeared in hundreds of period newspapers, both North and South, from 1861-1865. But the words of Douglass were especially significant for a variety of reasons. This is one of the early observations about Black Confederates and most famous quotes of Frederick Douglass, who has been the subject of a good many excellent biographies about America's foremost Black abolitionist leader both before and during the Civil War, including recent ones. How such a notable example can be overlooked by any historian is almost incomprehensible, because it was so well-known and often quoted by generations of Civil War historians.

In fact and truthfully, no search whatsoever for Black Confederates was even necessary or called for by Levin, who evidently conducted an imaginary or alleged quixotic search because the evidence of Black Confederates that exists today is so plentiful in the historical records, including primary sources like diaries, memoirs, and letters, including those from Union soldiers, and in almost too many historic accounts both primary and secondary during the war and postwar period to count. And today, more and more period photographs, tintypes and ambrotypes, have been found of Black Confederates in full uniforms of gray and even with weapons in their hands. Even more and based on Union eyewitness reports of men on the firing line, artist Theodore R. Davis produced a famous wartime sketch of armed Black Confederates who were members and fighting men of General Robert E. Lee's Army of Northern Virginia, when they were serving in the trenches of Petersburg, Virginia. Even more, this well-known sketch appeared prominently in the January 10, 1865 issue of *Harper's Weekly*, New York City, to prove a fundamental truth to the readers of the North about a undeniable reality about Black Confederate fighting men that had long existed, as confirmed by the historical record and plentiful primary and secondary sources.

Partial proof of these well-known historical realities about the existence of Black Confederate fighting men to any longtime student of the Civil War can be seen in on-target Amazon reviews by knowledgeable and educated readers, like J. H. Segars in February 2020 because he has written at length about Black Confederates, of Levin's book. These honest and truthful reviews have appropriate titles such as "Ignores Facts that do not Support his Thesis" (November 3, 2019) and "Written through a Political Lens and a Personal Agenda" (February 27, 2020). Mr. Segars, whose fine past works about Black Confederates goes back decades, correctly emphasized at the end of his Amazon review how: "Readers are smart enough to do their own research" that will quickly and easily reveal the presence of Black Confederates in gray uniforms (legitimate fighting men) during the war years from 1861 to 1865 and from beginning to end of the conflict. But perhaps Amazon reviewer Marie C. Ray Ford said it best in the title of her Amazon review for Levin's book on June 9, 2021: "Should be filed under 'Fiction'," given all the ample historical evidence that has revealed the considerable presence of Black Confederate fighting men from every state and in every Southern army on both sides of the Mississippi, especially the Army of Northern Virginia. Then, in the narrative of her review for *Searching for Black Confederates* that was right on target, Ford saved the best for last which could not have been more on-target: "So biased it's laughable." Again in an era when fake book reviews are often employed on the internet by liberals as I have experienced against my own books, including my 2018 *Blacks in Gray Uniforms*, by way of a recent investigation, these mentioned reviews are legitimate, true, and right on target from educated people and historians to reveal fundamental historical truths that simply cannot be denied, because they are backed up by the historical facts and truths.

To set the record straight about Black Confederates, Harvard University scholars said it best by emphasizing how the South employed between 3,000-6,000 fighting men in the ranks of Southern armies on both sides of the Mississippi River during the Civil War. Even on Levin's own personal blog of October 31, 2020, one critical reviewer wrote the "scary" and "frightening" truth on Halloween, appropriately enough: "LOL, you had that much trouble finding black Confederates? A one minute search on Google turns up plenty of credible evidence of their existence." Nevertheless, the book was preposterously entitled *Searching for Black Confederates* in a title that could not be more misleading to the American public, while declaring in the subtitle that Black fighting men are *The Civil War's Most Persistent Myth* in the very process of creating a new myth! Again, this is a classic case of turning the truth of history on its head and upside down, as noted by the critical and honest Amazon reviews of Levin's book that were right on target.

Quite simply, amazingly and in rather remarkable fashion, by attacking what he believes is a "myth" when it is certainly not at all the case given all of the ample existing historical evidence that says otherwise, author Levin created his own myth about the Civil War, like in the case of the much-touted and celebrated author of *The 1619*

Project. Clearly, this is an extremely sad and unfortunate testament about the state of the historical field in America today. Indeed, it has become fashionable today to create historical myths in the Age of Political Correctness to confirm with the dictates of popular and trendy political agendas of the Left and have them published which is a rather remarkable development in itself, even by respectable presses in America, at a time when Americans can no longer believe, and correctly so, what they read and hear stemming from the Left-leading modern media and their government in Washington, D.C. In what has been an inevitable development that has presented one of the saddest commentaries about the harmful and damaging effects of the spread of political correctness like a cancer, so why not fabricate history in such a receptive political environment at a time when truth has died in America and corruption has thrived in all aspects of American life, especially political? For the promoters of political correctness and many liberals, this unfortunate situation that now exists in America has presented an unprecedented opportunity for Left-leaning authors to foster historical untruths upon the American people for little more than recognition and profit.

Levin has promoted his new Civil War myth in media circles, the "rubber chicken" circuit, and schools to influence adults and young, formative minds since the release of his 2019 book, while propagandizing to American audiences in the Leftist tradition. In historical terms, this is not unlike Joseph Goebbels, the infamous

Nazi Chief of Propaganda in Berlin, in having repeatedly emphasized the "Big Lie": a classic case of how if a particularly outlandish lie is repeated enough in both written and spoken form, then it will be believed by the average person in America today, who simply does not know any better because they don't know their history, especially about Black Confederates and the truthful history about the South, including as the legacy of Black fighting men going all the way back to many years before the American Revolution, especially in the case of the often-threatened Colony of South Carolina.

Again, this unfortunate situation in America today is a classic case of the politization and mythologizing of history like in the case of *The 1619 Project,* because of Left-leaning agendas that are infamous for perverting and obstructing the truth, especially in history, for their own purposes not unlike the highly-effective propagandizing machines of Socialist and Communist governments around the world for decades. One of the first orders of business for a Communist or Socialist government coming to power has been a primary focus on the rewriting of history as infamously seen in the case with the Soviet Union and Communist China. And now Russia has put a new spun on Ukrainian history because of the Russian-Ukraine War in an attempt to erase the Ukrainian historical past, especially the longtime stirring of Ukrainian nationalism in the face of Russian dominance for centuries, for political reasons. Erasing and rewriting history has long been a core tenet of Communist and Socialist doctrine to enhance the power of the state and to minimize patriotic resistance to dictatorial rule.

For example, after the Republic of South Vietnam fell to the Communist forces of North Vietnam in April 1975 when America pulled out of the country and discontinued its longtime support of his Southeast Asia ally, one of the first missions of the victorious North Vietnamese was to send large numbers of South Vietnamese, especially former soldiers and government officials, to reeducation camps to instill their propaganda and agenda of the Communist Party: a comparable process that had become familiar in twenty-first century America that has slowly becoming more socialist over time and seemingly with each passing day, especially in the school systems and including colleges across the United States. These two recent books in question are a classic example of the rewriting of history that had first required the erasing of history like emphasizing that Black Confederates do not exist because they are a myth. This is like Communist and Socialist rewriting of history by reshaping history by rewriting the past to erase great nationalist and patriotic heroes and heroic liberation struggles.

Because of these unfortunate developments based on today's dictates of Left-leaning politics that have become so fashionable and trendy in America, I have decided that it is finally time to kindly assist Mr. Levin, who is a non-Ph.D. and who often lectures and performs before audiences (he has long described himself on his personal blog as a "Historian, Educator, Public Speaker") in his alleged diligent and dedicated search (I wonder if this has been a lifelong search as his book's title seems to have suggested?) for Black Confederates, since he evidently had a great deal of trouble finding any Black Confederates who fought for the South, although they can be found in a simple and brief Google search and throughout the historical records, especially period newspapers, North and South, and even including major newspapers in New York City. Levin's self-proclaimed title of "Educator" is significant because of its implications and true meaning. But is Levin actually educating by teaching wrong historical information that is largely politically based? The Communists and Socialists have long relied a twisting of historical truths, including "reeducation" camps, to emphasize their political agendas at the expense of historical truths. Of course, educating the public is always important and highly-commendable, but not if this process of education has been tainted because it has been politically driven at the expense of historical facts and realities. If so, then this is nothing more than political propaganda like in the old Soviet Union.

Based on the wording of his book's title, I know that Levin must be utterly mentally and physically exhausted from his long, arduous search year after year and I greatly sympathize with his sense of dedication in his tireless efforts in pursuit of these "elusive" Black Confederates, although this great search has allegedly failed to produce any results or evidence about Black fighting men in the South, when in fact they can easily be found by anyone, even by a child, on the internet today. As suggested by the book's title, Levin's search was evidently not unlike the medieval search by chivalric knights for the Holy Grail. Of course, this was the most famous Arthurian legend about the historic search for this fabled religious relic with allegedly miraculous healing powers. From the wording of the book's title, Levin's fruitless for Black Confederates has been much like the fruitless search for gold in Florida—there was none in the subtropical wilderness of the Florida peninsula—by the early Spanish explorers in the early 1500s.

I hope that Kevin can fully recover one day from his long and exhaustive search for historical information about Black fighting men that he was unable to find anywhere like Don Quixote searching in vain for glory or like the endless search of men for centuries attempting to find the tomb of Alexander the Great, which lies today somewhere under the vast urban sprawl of Alexandra, Egypt, and the crowded homes of its around 4 million people. But Levin should be applauded for his dauntless and quixotic (and even "brave") efforts under such exceedingly difficult, if not impossible, circumstances?) search for historical information about Black Confederate fighting men that he was unable to find anywhere, and he still evidently believes does not exist—the rather incredible, if not bizarre, thesis of his 2019 book--, as explained so proudly (an obvious pride in an abject failure as revealed in a title was quite extraordinary in itself) in the book's title. So, it truly must have been an epic search by Levin to have so boldly emphasized his great quest in

Searching for Black Confederates to reveal an allegedly Holy Grail-like pursuit of evidently almost epic proportions year after year like a true dedicated historian. So, Mr. Levin, who is still a relatively young man, should be honored today for the "heroic" diligence of his long search of a quixotic quest, despite yielding no results which speaks very highly of his sheer determination to find the historical truth at any cost, despite many years of experiencing frustration in his great quest of discovery.

The Unvarnished Truth That Cannot Be Denied

Clearly, as his book's title has revealed and suggested, then perhaps Levin should be ranked with the great explorers and searchers of history who bravely pursued their dreams, like Henry M. Stanley, a former Confederate soldier who fought at Shiloh, Tennessee, in early April 1862, who long searched for Scottish Dr. David Livingstone in Africa and finally found him in November 1871, or like the Crusaders of the Middle Ages who trekked all the way from western Europe and to the Holy Land in the Middle East in search of holy relics from the time of Jesus Christ. In order to assist Kevin Levin in his relentless search (too bad that it has proved entirely futile which must have been extremely frustrating, if not painful, for him) for Black Confederate fighting men, I have decided to write this current groundbreaking book entitled *Forgotten Black*

Confederate Fighting Men at the Battle of Painesville, Virginia, on April 5, 1863. This is the first book ever written about the first battle that was fought by a large, organized, and fully uniformed group of around 200, or more, Black fighting men, who served in a Confederate infantry command, a full battalion, that had been created by the national government at the capital in Richmond, Virginia in early 1865, at the forgotten Battle of Painesville, Virginia, on the morning of April 5, 1865, when the reeling Army of Northern Virginia was retreating west after the fall of Petersburg and Richmond, Virginia, when the Army of the Potomac under Ulysses S. Grant was in fast pursuit.

After much debate and argument in the Confederate Congress at Richmond, these ebony soldiers, both slaves and free men, had been recently recruited by two white officers in Richmond, after the Confederate Congress had belatedly approved the use of Black Confederates on March 13, 1865, but with no provisions for freedom of these slaves. Then, President Jefferson Davis, a Mexican-American War veteran from Mississippi who realized that the necessary next political step was required, issued a military order on March 22, 1865 that guaranteed the winning of freedom for enslaved Black Confederate troops, if they faithfully served, because he did not believe that the Confederate legislative would pass an act of manumission for these ebony soldiers, because of strong existing opposition in the Confederate Congress. Of course, in such a desperate situation, this measure was a last-ditch effort of the Confederate government to replenish the much-depleted manpower of the Army of Northern Virginia, which was the South's primary army in the Eastern Theater and now fighting for its life that was flickering away. But, of course, it was all too little, too late by this time, because the Confederate Government had acted much too late. The Black soldiers, both slaves and free men, of the Confederacy's first official two Black companies, or infantry battalion, consisted of around 200 ebony fighting men, both slave and free, or perhaps as many as 300 Black soldiers in the end, of regular soldiers in gray uniforms organized by the Richmond government. They were trained and disciplined by Majors Thomas P. Turner and Joseph W. Pegram, who was capable white officers with experience, at the nation's capital of Richmond, when the Civil War was finally drawing to a close in early 1865.

As fate would have it and quite by accident, the Confederacy's first official Black soldiers of a full battalion, or two companies, of the regular army were assigned a crucial role, although seemingly an inglorious one, near the end of the Civil War. When Richmond was evacuated on the night of April 2 after the Army of the Potomac had captured the strategic railroad center of Petersburg just to Richmond's south that had long supplied the capital and the Army of Northern Virginia to support their existence, the Black Confederate soldiers were ordered to escort and guard the crucial last supply wagon train—180 wagons—out of the evacuated Richmond that was ordered to unite with General Robert E. Lee's Army of Northern Virginia on the long and desperate retreat west to

Amelia Court House, southwest of Richmond. Here, General Lee had designated for the retreating forces from Richmond and Petersburg, which had been evacuated at the same time as the capital, to assemble in central Virginia, after the lengthy retreat from Petersburg and Richmond. At this time, the overall situation for the Confederacy, which was on the ropes as never before, could not have been more desperate. This was now a high stakes race west of the South's primary eastern army to escape the clutches of General Grant's pursuing army, especially its excellent cavalry arm under the hard-hitting General Phil Sheridan, who was Grant's best top cavalry lieutenant known for his aggressiveness and skill.

Therefore, with Petersburg and Richmond evacuated because they could no longer be held, it was now General Lee's most critical concern to make sure that his famished troops received supplies while they were on the move west toward the objective of Danville, Virginia, located just north of the North Carolina line. Most of all after the loss of Petersburg and Richmond that fell like dominoes, this was now a logistical war and General Lee needed a logistical miracle for the Army of Northern Virginia to survive and fight another day. Hence, the crucial importance of the last Confederate supply train of wagons dispatched from Richmond, because the army depended on the large amount of supplies that Lee had ordered to reach Amelia Court House, which the general, a Virginian and distinguished Mexican-American War veteran, had targeted as the place in central Virginia for his retreating army to secure his much-needed supplies that were eagerly anticipated from the arriving boxcars on the railroad to Danville. But these anticipated supplies by rail never arrived in a fatal bureaucratic mix-up that cost the reeling Army of Northern Virginia dearly in a time of crisis.

At the forgotten Battle of Painesville, Virginia, on the shiny morning of April 5, which was only 4 days before General Lee surrendered his battered Army of Northern Virginia to General Grant at Appomattox Court House, the well-trained and uniformed Black fighting men, under the command of Major Joseph W. Pegram, played the leading role in defending the main supply wagon train from the recently evacuated Richmond, when the wagons were attempting to reach Lee's main army converging at Amelia Court House. Here, in an impressive defensive stand for rookie Black soldiers to save the precious wagons of supplies so badly needed by the starving men of the Army of Northern Virginia just to the southeast of Painesville, they repulsed the sweeping charge of the battle-hardened veterans of the 1st New Jersey Cavalry, despite being rookies and novices at war. This fine Federal command was an excellent experienced combat regiment consisting of hardy veterans headed by a most promising commander, twenty-two-year-old Colonel Hugh Hartshorne Janeway. The dynamic, hard-charging Janeway was fated to be later killed later in the day on April 5 in courageously leading another cavalry charge at Amelia Court House. The climactic showdown at Painesville, which was located only four miles northwest of Amelia Court House in western

Amelia County, in which the Black Confederate troops protected the 180 supply wagons was a dramatic one, because the stakes were exceptionally high for the Army of Northern Virginia and the Confederacy, which was on the ropes as never before: General Lee desperately needed the precious supplies, especially rations for his famished Southern soldiers, because he had found none of the expected rations in the boxcars of the train that had been sent from Richmond, which had arrived at Amelia Court House. However, bureaucratic mistakes and confusion ensured that the ration's arrival never happened as Lee had expected and ordered.

The dramatic showdown at Painesville first began on the bright, spring morning of April 5 in the Virginia Piedmont, when Sheridan directed General George Crook to dispatch forward the veteran cavalry brigade of Brigadier General Henry E. Davies. Davies then discovered the immense wagon train of General Custis Lee sent from Richmond situated just outside the small town of Painesville, Virginia: a certain guarantee that a battle was about to be fought because the top priority of the Union cavalry pursuers was to deny Lee's reeling army of supplies and attack any Confederate troops in sight. The New Jersey regiment, under capable Colonel Hugh Janeway who was one of Crook's top lieutenants, formed for the attack on an open hill, which overlooked the lengthy expanse of the wagon train situated on lower ground, around 10:00 am on April 5. The sweeping cavalry charge of one of the finest cavalry regiments of the Army of the Potomac was only moments away.

Then, all of a sudden, Union officers from the Garden State shouted orders and bugles sounded the charge, which caused the Black Confederate soldiers, who were wearing new and smart uniform of gray, to hurriedly form for action behind a light breastwork to defend the large wagon train, as they had been taught by white officers during training at Richmond. These minted soldiers of African descent were eager to prove their worth and manhood and shatter ugly racial stereotypes, because many of these rookie soldiers (the ones who were not free men who had willingly volunteered to defend the South) had been slaves only a relatively short time before. For the first time, the Black Confederates of a full infantry battalion were about to meet the Yankees, who had invaded their Southern homeland with fire and sword.

The Black Confederate soldiers in neat gray uniforms quickly prepared to fight from behind the excellent cover of the light earthworks, which already had been strengthened by them with fence rails atop the earthen parapet, that they had created to protect the supply wagons, to bestow greater confidence among the ebony fighting men in their first battle. Enfield muskets, which had been imported through the Union naval blockade from England, were checked one last time along with leather cartridge-boxes, that contained forty rounds, by the sides of the Black Confederates. Significantly, this morning showdown about two hours before noon was the first meeting on any battlefield between the largest organized group of Black soldiers formed by the Richmond government with the Yankees during the dramatic showdown at Painesville.

In this emergency situation among the gently rolling hills of western Amelia County, Virginia, the Black soldiers had used shovels and picks to create the light earthworks to protect the invaluable wagon train that had been sent from the nation's capital of Richmond, just before it fell. At a time when every fighting man was desperately needed in the ranks, these Black Confederates were the reliable escorts of the vital supply train, that was part of General Curtis Lee's column, which was the last one out of the evacuated Richmond. As mentioned, this increasingly important wagon train had been on its way to link with the Army of Northern Virginia at Amelia Court House, southwest of Richmond and southeast of Painesville, to provide the famished Southern army with invaluable supplies, because Lee's dissolving army would have to surrender, if it failed to receive supplies. But now the fast-moving Union cavalry had caught up with the supply train near Painesville northwest of Amelia Court House, which had now suddenly become important in this war for the first time.

The Confederacy's capital located along the muddy James River had just been evacuated on April 2, after General Grant, who brilliantly commanded the Army of the Potomac that was now achieving its greatest triumphs in this picturesque early spring, captured the strategic city of Petersburg, which was located just south of Richmond.

Petersburg's fall on the Appomattox River guaranteed the evacuation of the capital of Richmond because its last supply line was now severed by Petersburg's loss. After four bloody years and the loss of more than 600,000 American lives, the Civil War was coming to an end during this beautiful springtime in Virginia, after Union troops entered Richmond and Petersburg with flags flying in the early hours of April 3. Symbolically, Black troops, mostly former slaves of the United States Colored Troops (USCT), in blue uniforms were the first to enter Richmond and accept the surrender of the Confederacy's capital in a most symbolic gesture.

At this time, the last supply wagon train out of Richmond had been retreating southwest with the gray and butternut column of General Custis Lee, the son of Robert E. Lee, while pushing toward the fertile piedmont of central Virginia donned in spring colors from the recent rains. This was a desperate attempt of what little was left of the Army of Northern Virginia to organize and link with the main army that Lee had ordered to concentrate at Amelia Court House from both Richmond and Petersburg before it was too late with Grant's army, especially the large number of bluecoat cavalrymen under General Sheridan, in fast pursuit. Both the Army of Northern Virginia and the Confederacy were in their death throes in early April 1865, ensuring that Grant continued to demand a vigorous pursuit by his troops, both infantry and cavalry, while envisioning that the end was near for the fabled Army of Northern Virginia.

All the while on the morning of April 5 just northwest of Amelia Court House, where Lee's Army was attempting to concentrate and serving as the destination of the Southern wagon train with Custis Lee's column from Richmond, the Black Confederates, including one or two men of a color sergeant's rank who carried Confederate flags, were ready for action, when the inevitable Union cavalry attack was finally unleashed. They watched silently with cocked muskets as the bluecoat troopers of the 1st New Jersey Cavalry Regiment launched their charge from the high ground and straight toward the massive wagon train, which contained tons of invaluable supplies and munitions so badly needed for Lee's Army, which was steadily retreating west to escape Grant's clutches, to survive and fight another day to continue America's bloodiest war, when the Confederacy's life was at stake.

If the Black Confederate soldiers, who were not assisted by white soldiers except their own officers—meanwhile, on the other side, the Black troops of the United States Colored Troops (USCT) fighting for the Union also had white officers who commanded them—failed to hold firm under the mounted onslaught, then disaster would result. If successful, they would be playing a key role in attempting to save the day by ensuring that the invaluable supplies for Lee's starving army eventually got through to General Lee at Amelia Court House and reached what little was left of the decimated Army of Northern Virginia. As noted, the arrival of the main supply train, escorted by the Black Confederates, from Richmond would immeasurably lift the sagging morale of General Lee's hungry and foot-weary soldiers during the long retreat west, while they correctly feared that the end of the army's life was near and desertions from the ranks increased accordingly.

And the end would be much nearer for General Lee and what relatively little was left of the Army of Northern Virginia if this main wagon supply train, drawn by slow-moving mules since all horses were used by the Confederate cavalry, from Richmond was captured by Union cavalry, if the Black soldiers demonstrated cowardice or failed in their vital mission of defending the main Confederate wagon train and its crucial supplies and munitions from the capital on the James River to the northeast. With flashing sabers, hundreds of New Jersey troopers swarmed down from the high ground toward this thin line of Black Confederate troops crouching in good firing positions in their light breastworks and holding firm for nerve-racking minutes, while the pounding hooves of an avalanche of hundreds of horses sounded like thunder. Meanwhile, the brass cavalry bugles of the bluecoat troopers split the spring air with piercing notes that slanted over the colorful Virginia woodlands consisting of blooming redbuds and the white blossomed dogwood trees scattered across the vibrant green landscape of the Virginia Piedmont, which had been recently nourished by soft, warm spring rains, around what was called Paines Cross Roads, or Painesville, located just northwest of Amelia Court House.

Incredibly, the around 200 ebony fighting men, or more, and consisting of an entire infantry battalion of trained soldiers in gray uniforms, still held firm in the face of the fierce Union cavalry attack. The new Black Confederates were simply not acting like this was their first battle, displaying high morale and a determination to stand up against the fierce Union cavalry charge. To the credit of these newest soldiers of the Confederacy, no one in the ranks of the Black infantrymen panicked and ran off from their assigned defensive position at the light earthworks, which was so often the case of rookie soldiers in the first battle and when under their first cavalry attack during the Civil War. Instead, the Black Confederates calmly and gamely remained in their advanced position behind the light breastworks, aiming a solid row of muskets at the charging troops from New Jersey, while they maintained their courage and composure in a highly tense, anxious situation. When hundreds of New Jersey cavalrymen, with sabers flashing in the early April sunshine, neared the lengthy line of Black Confederate soldiers, the ebony defenders of the wagon train still remained defiantly and solidly in position, refusing to budge an inch. All the while, they waited quietly for Major Joseph W. Pegram and their other white officers to order these novice soldiers to open fire during their supreme moment of truth that had come at long last not far from the small town of Painesville.

After all, these stoic men of African descent, except for the free Blacks in the ranks, had been slaves who worked mostly in the fields and also in the Confederate hospitals in

Richmond, before the Confederate Congress finally passed the law on March 13 to form Black Confederate units of fighting men for service in the army and then President Davis had guaranteed them freedom for loyal service by an executive order on March 22. And now near the rural village of Painesville, Virginia, the greatest challenge in the lives of these Black men now existed for them to play a key role and demonstrate their manhood and equality to white soldiers, both Union and Confederate, had finally come at long last. Then, with the New Jersey troopers of the 1st Brigade, 2nd Division, Army of the Potomac, charging near and too close for comfort, the white Rebel officers, who were experienced leaders, of the Black Confederate troops at last ordered their men, who were mostly from the State of Virginia, to open fire, when it seemed as if the Yankee cavalry on their big horses thundering toward them were so close that they could almost be touched.

A thunderous volley from hundreds of Enfield rifles finally exploded from the long line of Black soldiers positioned from behind the earthworks and it was a devastating one. Numerous New Jersey troopers tumbled off their horses, which also went down in the confusion and tumult. The close-range volley was too scorching hot even for these veteran cavalrymen of the Army of the Potomac. The New Jersey men immediately turned their horses and retreated back to the safety of the high ground to escape the punishing fire in some disorder not expected from a veteran regiment known for its high quality and reliability on the battlefield. Clearly, this was a most historic battle fought among the gently rolling piedmont hills in western Amelia County southwest of Richmond—the first ever fought by a large, organized group of Black Confederate soldiers of a full infantry battalion that had been created by the Richmond government. In the process and at least initially, the Black Confederate troops won their first fight at Painesville, while shattering the endless racial stereotypes and myths about the inferiority of Blacks, especially the most pervasive ones that they lacked courage and character to fight bravely like white men—one of the longest-lasting and greatest of all racial myths in American history: the racial falsehoods and myths that had long served as a central foundation of racism, prejudice, and discrimination to justify slavery for centuries.

The bloodied New Jersey troopers of Colonel Janeway's punished regiment had learned their lesson well and the hard way that they should not have underestimated the ebony soldiers, because the bodies of dead and wounded New Jersey boys lay scattered on the ground, after the Union bugles had sounded the retreat. This, of course, was a verification of the courage and tenacity of the Black Confederate soldiers in the heat of combat, when they proudly wore their new uniforms of gray at the forgotten Battle of Painesville, Virginia, on the picturesque morning of April 5, 1865. However, after having been reinforced, Colonel Janeway and his 1st New Jersey Regiment then joined in the next and much larger Union cavalry attack with the entire brigade that broke through the thin, gray defensive line and shattered the Black and white Confederates of General Custis Lee's column on this forgotten battlefield near the rural village of Painesville.

A Forgotten Distinguished Legacy

As mentioned, this current book has been largely written not only in pursuit of the truth in history but also for the personal benefit of author Kevin M. Levin to convince him that he perhaps should have been more diligent in his epic search (based on his book's title) for Black Confederates, because he somehow experienced considerable difficulty in finding any Black Confederate soldiers at all, although they can be found practically everywhere by just a brief search of the internet that even a child could conduct in short order. However, the role of Black Confederates at the Battle of Painesville on April 5, 1865 has been forgotten and overlooked to this day: the genesis for the writing of this current book. Even a fine oil painting, which was published in a popular 2015 book—four years before the publication of Levin's book--by distinguished publisher Osprey Publishing, Ltd., which is one of the world's leading military publishers, even portrayed for the first time ever the spirited defense of the Black Confederates in gray uniforms protecting the main supply train from Richmond from their defensive position near Painesville on April 5, 1865, which has been presented in a colorful graphic form. At this time and as fully demonstrated near Painesville in the Virginia Piedmont of western Amelia County, these forgotten Black Confederates, consisting of both slaves and free black fighting men, of an entire infantry battalion were more than willing to sacrifice their lives for the Confederacy in fulfilling their assignment of defending the wagon train so badly needed by Lee's army. No white officer had forced these around 200, or even more, ebony fighting men of two companies of an entire infantry battalion to defend the earthworks in the face of the fierce cavalry charge of the New Jersey troopers, because they believed that they were defending their sacred homeland from Yankee invaders and a nascent sense of Southern nationalism like in the case of all people, when they have become victims of what they considered to be the aggression and imperialism of a "foreign" invader since time immemorial.

So, this current 2023 book, which is the first-ever one devoted the story of the distinguished role and tenacious defense of the Black Confederate troops at the Battle of Painesville on April 5, 1865, will certainly help to enlightened Americans, including Kevin M. Levin who must still be completely exhausted from his long, arduous search of Black Confederate fighting men that evidently took many years of strenuous effort and struggle against the odds based on his book's title. For the first time, I have illuminated this forgotten chapter of the Civil War about the key contributions of a full infantry battalion of Black Confederate fighting men at the Battle of Painesville. Somehow in all of his searching, Levin overlooked the dramatic story of the Battle of Painesville, although it was one of the last battles of the Civil War and famed Civil War newspaper artist Alfred Waud even sketched the battle at the time, in the most decisive and important campaign (Appomattox Campaign) of the Civil War and despite the fact that artist Adam Hook's fine painting fully revealed the courageous defensive stand of the Black Confederates troops in the excellent 2015 book that was published by a respected British publisher, Osprey Publishing, Inc., for an international audience. This fine book has continued to be sold today on both sides of the Atlantic to this day. Hopefully, Mr. Levin will purchase a copy so that his search might come to an end.

It is unfortunate that Levin missed everything about the Battle of Painesville and so much other ample existing evidence about Black Confederate fighting men in gray uniforms, as fully revealed and demonstrated in my 2018 book *Blacks in Gray Uniforms, A New Look at the South's Most Forgotten Combat Troops 1861-1865* and this current 2023 book about what happened on the morning of April 5, 1865 in western Amelia County, Virginia. Of course, my well-received book *Blacks in Gray Uniforms*, which was released about a year before the Levin book, was politically incorrect in this current so-called "Progressive" era of *The 1619 Project,* because it was based on the historical facts and truths and, most important, without any political agenda involved whatsoever. What my 2018 book proved in no uncertain terms was that there was no real search required at all to find Black Confederate fighting men, as alleged by the entirely misleading title of Levin's book, to mock his book's main thesis of a great search, which could not be more ahistorical and bogus.

Writing historical fiction and a false narrative based primarily on political agendas and the fashionable dictates of political correctness, like in the case of *The 1619 Project* and *Searching for Black Confederates*, is hardly a good way to establish one's credibility, while attempting to establish themselves in the historical field at the expense of fundamental historical facts and truths: the antithesis of what has always been accepted as normal practice and procedure in academe, the publishing field, and in the field of history for centuries. Longtime students of the Civil War already knew all about Black Confederate fighting men long before Levin was born in 1969 at the height of the Vietnam War and before he allegedly conducted his epic search that must have been extremely frustrating, because he was unable to find any evidence after years of searching like Don Quixote.

Because of the abundance of historical information and documentation, both primary and secondary, about the existence of Black Confederate fighting men, this situation begs the evidently never asked question by the publisher: was there even a search at all as emphasized in the book's very title? The peer review of the manuscript by the publisher should have early noticed this great discrepancy to have revealed the undeniable reality that in fact no search was at all necessary because so many examples of Black Confederates in combat roles can be easily found both on the internet and historical documents and primary sources, especially period newspapers. Quite simply, this incredible title of "searching" could not have been more misleading to fool the reading public about the fundamental truths and facts of American and Southern history when it comes to the subject of Black Confederate fighting men.

Again and as mentioned, there needed to be no search at all by Levin or anyone else for Black Confederate fighting men, because they can be found in hundreds of solid historical sources and documentation, including period newspapers and soldier (both Union and Confederate) letters, diaries, and memoirs, and these are historical realities and facts that cannot be overlooked or denied by the false creation of a new ahistorical myth based on the dictates of political correctness, because the evidence of Black Confederates is so pervasive, if not very nearly overwhelming, in the historical records and primary source documents. And even this small sample size of perhaps as many as 200, or more, Black Confederate fighting men of a full infantry battalion, who served with distinction in defense of the main Confederate supply wagon train from Richmond near Painesville on April 5, 1865, has proved and verified at much. Adam Hook's fine painting of Black Confederate fighting men in action near Painesville can be found in the excellent 2015 Osprey Publishing book entitled *Appomattox 1865, Lee's Last Campaign* by Ron Field. This groundbreaking painting created by talented artist Adam Hook that appears on pages 56-59 of the Osprey book has depicted more than 30 ebony warriors (a considerable underestimation due to artistic license and low-ball representation of the actual number of Black Confederates of the two-company battalion, who were engaged in the battle that April morning) in action in an only partial scene of the battle, while bravely repulsing the attack of the 1st New Jersey Cavalry Regiment, Army of the Potomac, in their first battle—no small accomplishment for rookie soldiers without prior battle experience.

In addition, Mr. Hook certainly should be commended for having the courage to depict Black Confederates in action—the first artist with the considerable nerve to do so especially in these days of political correctness--, which is something that average American artists would never do under the circumstances of today's political correctness and culture wars, which have continued to rage to this day. Fortunately, however, Hook is a British citizen, who has emerged today as one of finest military artists in the western world. All in all, this situation was a significant guarantee that he was far less contaminated by America's trendy dictates of political correctness that have intimated and cowed so many people, including politicians, historians, publishers, and artists, around the United States, while benefitting crass and shameless exploiters of the nation's dominant political mood. In consequence, Hook was able to depict a historically accurate painting based on historical facts rather than the current mood of political correctness that has dominated the United States, including even the school systems, for so long.

All in all, this current book, entitled *The Forgotten Black Confederate Fighting Men at the Battle of Painesville, April 5, 1865,* is most of all a myth busting work to expose the fraudulency of Kevin M. Levin's book, including others, and its misleading and quite ridiculous title of *Searching for Black Confederates* and then to have the considerable chutzpah to label the Black Confederates in the subtitle as *The Civil War's Most Persistent Myth,* when in truth there is actually no myth at all, except in Levin's mind and evidently that of his literary agent if that might have been the case, and that no real search was required at all to find Black men fighting for the Confederacy, because they exist countless times in many different primary and second sources, since they can be found almost anywhere one looks in historical records, both North and South and especially primary sources, such as period newspapers from across the South and also from the North, including New York City.

In this regard and what cannot be denied is the fact that few book titles have been more misleading and wrong-headed on every possible level, since it was evidently deliberately worded to generate publicity and sales, as if suggested by a media expert or literary agent without much historical knowledge. So, perhaps Levin is not entirely to blame for one of the most misleading of possible book titles in recent memory. All in all, this has been an unfortunate development in the field of history because it has revealed one of the extreme negative consequences of the Age of Political Correctness. Today, Americans have accepted the fact that their national leaders, including President Joseph R. Biden, whose family has racked in millions of dollars in bribes, including from Communist China, are corrupt and continuously lie to them from the entrenched mire of the deep cesspool that is everyday political life in the nation's capital in Washington, D.C., which has revealed today's unsavory environment in which even the facts of history can be similarly distorted and twisted for political reasons. In consequence, this current book, like my 2018 book *Blacks in Gray Uniforms, A New Look at the South's Most Forgotten Combat Troops 1861-1865*, has been written as a corrective work to counter the deliberate lies, myths, distortions, and falsehoods to reveal fundamental historical truths that have been grossly perverted by the dictates of political correctness, including to this day.

As this current book has demonstrated and proven in full like in my 2018 book *Blacks in Gray Uniforms*, this newly created myth about the alleged inability of a "historian" to find any Black Confederate combat troops in pure baloney from a historical point of view and sufficiently to the point of being laughable to a degree not found regarding any other book about the Civil War in the last half century. Quite simply, no myth could be more wrong-headed than the alleged non-existence of Black Confederate fighting men, as the abundant historical facts and documents have clearly proven to one and all, because even a child can find them on the internet. An October 2019 Amazon reviewer of Levin's book was right on target by emphasizing how it: "Ignores actual accounts of hundreds" of people on both sides during the war years of 1861-1865. Again, regarding Levin's book, J. H. Segars perhaps said it best in his 2020 Amazon review in which he stated the basic truth about how the American people "are smart enough to do their own research" from the abundance of historical accounts that have revealed the undeniable truth about the existence of Black Confederate fighting men from the beginning in 1861 to the very end in 1865. Like in my first book about Black Confederates, *Blacks in Gray Uniforms*, it is again time tell the unvarnished and well-documented truth about the remarkable story of Black Confederate fighting men on the battlefield, while busting the latest artificially created myth about their nonexistence. Attempting to prove that Black Confederates from 1861 to 1865 did not exist is almost like trying to prove that the Irish, Hebrews, Scots, Swedes, or Germans failed to fight for either side, because nothing could be farther from the truth. Any wrong-headed ahistorical attempt to deny fundamental truths in Civil War history has been nothing less than scandalous and shameful on many levels.

 Significantly, this current book has revealed that Black Confederates solders fought and died for the Confederacy in numbers that have been long either totally ignored or minimized by many of today's self-serving historians, who have embraced the ahistorical faith of political correctness with an unbridled passion at the expense of the existence of an ample amount of the historical facts and truths to gain either personal fame, recognition, or profits as authors. In consequence, this current book has been written to overturn the establishment and growth of the latest popular ahistorical myth, as perpetuated by Levin, based on the popular axioms of political correctness, while revealing historical facts and the truths that are undeniable. Of course and most of all, history should not be about creating a new myth to conform to the dictates of politics, especially political correctness, like the case of *The 1619 Project* and *Searching for Black Confederates.*

Unfortunately, educated historians, especially those who hold a Ph.D., in history, are much too knowledgeable and sensible today to embrace such new fantastic myths that have been created without historical foundation and substance because of politics, which has explained why *The 1619 Project* has been routinely dismissed out-of-hand by America's leading historians and academics. But, unfortunately, this is not the case with the American people, especially younger people who are vulnerable to lies, distortions of history, and falsehoods, just like Nazi leadership, especially the sinister Joseph Goebbels, knew exactly how to exploit and manipulate an entire generation of people, especially the young, to become devoted Nazis who were programed by years of propaganda and lies to be killed by the tens of thousands on battlefields, especially in the great killing fields of Russia, far from home and around the world for a fake and corrupt racist ideology of Aryan superiority and right to rule the world that had no validity or substance whatever: as silly and ahistorical of a concept as the alleged nonexistence of Black Confederates.

Hence, the importance today of thoroughly refuting the creation of new lies and new myths in American history, especially if politically-based like the Nazi lies that so thoroughly brainwashed the German people, especially children, before they can inflict too much damage to the thinking of naive people, especially younger persons who have been brainwashed by liberalism or so-called "progressivism," including from the pen of historian Howard Zinn, a self-proclaimed "Marxist" who wrote *A People's History of the United States*. All in all, Zinn's book is basically a socialist take on America's history. Most of all today, the American people certainly deserve better today by learning the truth about their history, especially African Americans whose rich history has been neglected for so long, without having been distorted and corrupted by the dictates of political correctness and certainly not the creation of new myths and ahistorical ones like in the notable cases of *The 1619 Project* and *Searching for Black Confederates*. Black Confederate fighting men demonstrated courage and character year after year and that should not be forgotten by Americans, both black and white, today: the genesis for the writing of this current book about the around 200, perhaps more, Black Confederates who fought with courage at the Battle of Painesville on the morning of April 5, 1865.

Ahistorical and self-serving myths that have been only recently created because of the self-serving dictates of the nation's political mood of political correctness certainly need today to be addressed and busted for the good of the nation and Americans, both black and white, in general, which I have attempted to accomplish with both my 2018 book and this current work. So, most of all, my *The Forgotten Black Confederate Fighting Men at the Battle of Painesville, April 5, 1865* has been written to drive another stake, like my 2018 book *Blacks in Gray Uniforms*, into the heart of a newly created myth that is an entirely false one that has festered and is damaging to Americans, especially today's youth, on multiple levels. The American people, especially young people, certainly deserve much better from the nation's historians than having to become victims of political agendas and propaganda in history. To their everlasting credit, Americans are more intelligent than to believe politically based new myths that are ahistorical and absurd, as if Homer was still writing his ancient stories, including tall tales about Achilles and other ancient heroes, about the Trojan War, when there were very few historical documents to verify what he had written in the pages of the *Iliad*.

Politically correct warriors Nikole Hannah-Jones and Kevin Levin of today's culture wars, which have raged with partisan bitterness, have created new myths to exploit not only today's gullible youth in America, but also the pervasive politically correct environment at the expense of true history and the historical facts, when in reality their books would have never been published only a relatively few years ago, because of these fundamental politically-based reasons that have descended upon an unsuspecting America like a locust plague. Contrary to the creation of

Levin's recent myth and as mentioned and as fully revealed in the two books written by this current author, there were large numbers of Black Confederate fighting men who served from 1861-1865 and this current book about the Battle of Painesville is the final and most forgotten chapter in the saga of Black Confederate soldiers, who served the South because it was their homeland and they were defending it against an aggressive invader: in truth, only the tip of the iceberg in the story of Black Confederate fighting men that began in the war's beginning as soon as Southern cannon fired on Fort Sumter, in Charleston's Harbor in mid-April 1861.

Indeed, and as mentioned, only today in this perverse and distorted age of political correctness when factual American history has been turned upside down would a book like *Searching for Black Confederates* be published at all, because it has only fostered a myth and a lie that has nothing to do with the truth and history, while the very antithesis of those two qualities so essential to the writing of good and honest history. A bogus "search" (as emphasized in the book's title to fool and bamboozle the American public) should never be grounds for the creation of new ahistorical myth, because it has come alarmingly close to serving as nothing more than political propaganda at the expense of history, including courageous Black fighting men who compiled a distinguished record of service to the Confederacy year after year, like at the Battle of Painesville. Consequently, this current book, released in 2023, has been written to right a great historical wrong that has been committed in the field of history by presenting the unvarnished historical truth to dismantle a newly minted and fabricated myth that was created in 2019 by Levin, who had no Ph.D. or the proper academic credentials to even begin to start attempting to fool the American public by creating historical myths without any historical foundation and those based on today's twisted dictates of political correctness. The chutzpah to even have attempted such an endeavor has bordered on the unbelievable and quite incredible. But history should be much more than simply about chutzpah.

To additionally assist Levin in his arduous search that I am assuming has evidently continued to this day like the relentless quest of fabled knights for the Holy Grail, I have included some legitimate and historical images of Black Confederates on this cover of this book, just in case he still refuses to believe the fundamental and undeniable truths about Black Confederates that have been revealed in full in my two books and can be found across the interest and in so many historical sources, both primary and secondary.

In consequence, this current book, entitled *The Forgotten Black Confederate Fighting Men at the Battle of Painesville, Virginia, April 5, 1865*, has been written not only to set the historical record straight about Black Confederates, but also to reveal the courage and character of those Black Confederates who bravely fought and died against the "foreign" invaders of their Southern homeland just like white Confederates, because of the existence of a nascent Southern nationalism and the dream of a better life for themselves and their families in the future. These ebony fighting men in gray uniforms at the Battle of Painesville near the war's end could have deserted in the face of the enemy, but they faithfully stayed in the ranks of their two companies of a full Confederate infantry battalion and fought to the very end, although the Civil War was over for all practical purposes by April 5, 1865. The forgotten Battle of Painesville fully demonstrated the bravery of a large number of Black Confederates, both slaves and free Blacks, of an entire battalion in a time of crisis and in an emergency situation for the lives of the Army of Northern Virginia and the Confederacy, when a great deal was at stake for their Southern nation.

Most of all, it is now time for the fundamental truths about Black Confederates to be revealed in full to counter the new ahistorical myths that have been created in the Age of Political Correctness and America's most unheroic age, which is the most ahistorical periods in the annals of American history at a time when historical facts and realities have become meaningless and obsolete in the name of political correctness. In 2018, my groundbreaking book, *Blacks in Gray Uniforms, A New Look at the South's Most Forgotten Combat Troops 1861-1865* set the historical record straight, but I decided that more work was needed at this time and as a rebuttal to the Levin book and his epic search. In this well-received 2018 volume, I emphasized the fundamental truths about Black Confederates and their importance and meaning in America's story, but I did not take a look at the Battle of Painesville, on April 5, 1865 for a variety of reasons.

In consequence, this current book has been written to address this earlier negligence on my part (my mistake) and to tell the forgotten story of the largest number of Black Confederates who fought together as an official combat unit, a full battalion of infantry, of the Confederacy during the last days of the Civil War. This is a dramatic and important story that needs to be told today in this distorted and perverse Age of Political Correctness—the first book ever written about the Battle of Painesville and the unforgettable role of the around 200, or more, Black Confederates, who fought in western Amelia County, Virginia, on the morning of April 5, 1865. As noted, this is a significant story because the Black men in gray uniforms who fought at Painesville were only the tip of the iceberg of the thousands of Black Confederates who fought for the Confederacy as fighting men in defense of their homeland against the invaders from the North from 1861 to 1865. According to the best figures of the experts, including Harvard University scholars, an estimated 3,000-6000 Black Confederates, both slave and free, fought for the Confederacy. And as noted, around 200 Black Confederates, but perhaps as many as 300 although that highest estimate number cannot be confirmed today, of a full infantry battalion who fought at the Battle of Painesville. However, because the story of Black Confederates has become the most politicized chapter and a true political" football" today in Civil War history, a concerted effort has been made by the liberal media machine and authors to deny the existence of Black Confederates in what has been an outrageous and egregious whitewashing of history in the creation of a new myth about their alleged non-existence, which could not be farther from the historical truth as revealed in this 2023 book and in my 2018 book about Black Confederate fighting men.

Both this current book and my 2018 book were written to give full credit and long deserved recognition to the forgotten Black soldiers who fought for the Confederacy, including at the Battle of Painesville on the morning of April 5, 1865, in what has become the most forgotten and overlooked chapter in the annals of Civil War history. Even more, this current book has provided some of the best evidence to thoroughly discredit and dismiss the popular and fashionable Black Confederate soldier deniers, who are not unlike Holocaust deniers because of their ahistorical emphasis and attempts to deny historical truths, who have thrived today for political reasons that have nothing at all to do with the historical facts and well-documented history about America's Civil War and greatest national crisis.

Phillip Thomas Tucker, Ph.D.
Central Florida
August 1, 2023

Chapter I

Forgotten Black Valor
From America's Beginning

Contrary to common belief today that has become popular in the United States, the institution of slavery was not America's original sin, because it had been inherited from the mother country, England. The British Empire grew wealthy in part from the great profits reaped from the lucrative slave trade long before the outbreak of the American Revolution at Lexington and Concord, Massachusetts, on April 19, 1775. Of course, slavery had been part of the human condition ever since the first humans went to war and then realized that it was more advantageous for them to make slaves of captured enemies instead of killing them outright. Then, industrial scale slavery was created in ancient times when entire cities and empires were attacked for the express purpose of securing slaves, especially young women for carnal pleasure. This was one of the forgotten reasons that caused the Trojan War in which the beauty of Helen has only served as a popular metaphor for the ancient warrior's powerful motivation of securing slave women by the invading ancient Greeks.

Homer depicted the endless squabbling among Greek warriors, including Archilles, over the prizes of the most beautiful slave women, presenting a realistic view of ancient warfare without the glory and the more mundane realities, especially for women who had been captured.

In fact, the very foundations of the great ancient civilizations of Greece and Rome, including some of the most magnificent ancient architecture ever created by man, were built on the sturdy foundation of a robust system of slavery, just like in the overall making of America, including westward expansion toward the setting sun. Leading to his rise to power and reputation that made him famous as one of history's greatest military commanders, Julius Caesar conquered Gaul (today's France from 58 BC to 50 BC) with his seemingly invincible Roman legions in one arduous campaign after another: a brutal and relentless conquest that sent hundreds of thousands of Gauls, who were mostly members of Celtic tribes, to the lucrative slave markets of Rome, which made him a wealthy and powerful man. Victorious Roman armies even marched into Rome with long columns of captives in front for display, while vast crowds cheered the sight. The case can be made that the extensive Roman conquests and great imperialist expansive—first in Italy and then around the world--were based in large part on securing slaves to sell on the auction block in Rome to reap fortunes for aggressive commanders and political leaders, while slaves served as the economic foundation—cheap labor—of the sprawling empire that had conquered most of the known world. This was the forgotten side of the much-touted majesty of the Roman Empire, which is still celebrated and admired to this day by people around the world.

Significantly, slaves were freed by the ancient Greeks and Romans to fight the enemies of their city-states and empire, respectively, and to defend their societies in times of crisis just like the desperate Confederacy in early 1865. Ancient Sparta only became a thorough and complete warrior society devoted totally to the ways of war because of their society's dependence on their large slave population to work the fields and to do all the domestic labor which had then released Spartan fighting men from the fields, the Helots. They were a people who had been early conquered by Spartan imperialism, aggressiveness, and expansion. Because Spartan men could totally concentrate on the art of waging war, they had no equals in the ancient world as warriors. For such reasons, the most famous last stand in the annals of western history at Thermopylae in 480 BC was distinguished by the fierce fighting of not only the 300 Spartans of King Leonidas' elite bodyguard, but also hundreds of Helots, because each warrior had Helots to attend him. What has been most forgotten about the famous Battle of Thermopylae was that a large number of slaves also defended the strategic "Hot Gates" against the tide of Eastern warriors, including Ethiopians, from the vast Persian Empire under King Xerxes, dying beside the Spartan masters who were cut down to the last man in the most fabled last stand in the annals of western history: the most forgotten story about the famous showdown between East and West at Thermopylae.

In the beginning of America's settlement in the New World, slavery was as thriving of an institution in early New England as in the South, if not more so. Today, the story of the vibrancy of the institution of slavery in New England has been largely forgotten by Americans, because most people naturally associate slavery with the antebellum South and cotton cultivation (the primary focus of generations of American historians) during the era when "Cotton was King" to fuel not only the Southern, but also the American economy for generations. Even more, it was mostly New England's large merchant fleet of vessels that carried slaves across the Atlantic during the hellish "Middle Passage" and brought slaves to the South, especially to the largest slave trading port of Charles Town, South Carolina, which became Charleston after the American Revolution was won in 1783. New England shippers long profited from the vibrant slave trade, which also helped to make New England a wealthy, prosperous, and powerful region that was far more powerful than the South as demonstrated during the outcome of the Civil War. The welfare and development of America rested solidly on slavery like overall western progress and development, including Europe.

The American colonies were part of the vast international system and thriving industry that was slavery, profiting immensely from the suffering of others and growing rich in the process. Quite simply, early America would not have become prosperous without a robust system of slavery. For centuries, every major European power and their colonies benefitted from the cheap labor of African slaves, which helped to make them prosperous, wealthy, and powerful. Europe, America, and Africa were closely and solidly linked together in a vast network by the lucrative business of slavery. Even Africa benefitted, because tribal economies thrived from the capture and trading of large numbers of fellow Africans to the European slave traders, who were always eager buyers.

Quite simply, the success of the thirteen English colonies rested solidly on the foundation of slavery and it was vital to America from the beginning, because it was so successful and profitable. European powers waged wars to secure the profitable slave colonies, especially in the Caribbean when sugar was the greatest cash crop in the world, of their rivals. Quite simply, slavery made the eighteenth and nineteenth century worlds go around, producing cash crops of coffee, sugar, tobacco and finally cotton that produced fantastic wealth. More than twelve million Africans were sent across the hellish "Middle Passage" from Africa, coming to the Americas in chains, with eleven million surviving the nightmarish journey, because the entire system rested and thrived on the exploitation of enslaved Africans. Although America won its independence from Great Britain, whose slave port cities, like London, Liverpool, and Bristol, became rich, which had become powerful partly from the profits repeated the lucrative slave trade, in 1783 and despite the republic's egalitarian founding principles that "all men are created equal," slavery continued to be warmly embraced by generations of Americans because of its economic profitability and hardly any voice was raised in opposition from the beginning of the world's most profitable institution.

Despite the world's most horrendous institution that was the greatest stain on the American republic and experiment in democracy, slaves in early America played forgotten roles in helping to tame the western and northern frontiers not only by their muscle and brawn in developing the land and producing the crops, but also serving, both voluntarily and impressed, in defense of isolated settler homes and communities during attacks of Native Americans from the New England frontier in the north to the Georgia frontier in the south for decades. During moments of crisis and danger, slaves were routinely armed by whites to fight enemies across America, resulting in the ultimate survival of some entire English colonies, especially South Carolina because it was located so close to the omnipresent threat of Spanish Florida during what was basically a continuation of old religious and economic rivalries and the religious wars of Protestantism against Catholicism that had been waged for centuries across Europe, including the Hundred Years' War.

From the late 1600s and through the Yamasee War of 1715-1717, slaves of South Carolina played vital roles in repulsing every attack that descended on the weak, vulnerable colony by Native Americans and the Spanish of Spanish Florida to the south. Blacks, including organized companies of armed fighting men, rose to the fore during the Yamasee War in which around 70% of the white population of the Colony of South Carolina was killed by Native Americans, ensuring that the situation was extremely desperate with the colony on the verge of extinction. This development of Black fighting men on American soil during the colonial period long before the American Revolution was also a natural one as it would be from 1775 to 1783 during the struggle for liberty. None of the armed activities and defensive capabilities of Blacks, both slave and free, in America during the eighteenth century should be surprising to anyone today, because Africans hailed from well-trained warrior societies located mostly in west Africa and most slaves had been captured by fellow Africans in African wars to become slaves in America. Most important, the fact that slaves were longtime defenders of America since long before the American Revolution is one of the most forgotten stories of America history, which has helped to verify that both black and white worked and fought together in the overall process of the building of America together from the beginning both in terms of settlement and defense of this new homeland: today, a politically-incorrect historical truth of the American experience from the beginning.

However, the Black sacrifices have been long forgotten and ignored by generations of white historians, who have been guilty of simply dismissing and ignoring Black history until around the 1960s, when America saw profound social changes so much for the better. In this context and in a very real sense, Black history is not really Black history at all, but in truth American history pure and simple. For instance, an estimated 7,000 Blacks, both slave and free, fought as Patriots, including sizeable numbers as Continentals, who were reliable regulars, in the ranks of General George Washington's Continental Army, including in the major battles of the American Revolution. For instance, an estimated 700 Blacks served in the hard-fought Battle of Monmouth, New Jersey, on June 28, 1778 during Washington's desperate attempt to destroy Sir Henry Clinton's army, when it was retreating northeast from the evacuated Philadelphia to New York City.

Black Patriot contributions began with the first clash of arms of the American Revolution. A slave of Benjamin Estabrook, Prince Estabrook, was one of these men who was the first to fight for America. He was a militiaman of Lexington, Massachusetts, when the British redcoats marched into the town on the morning of April 19, 1775 on their way to Concord to the west to confiscate hidden arms and munitions of the Patriots. When the first battle that ignited the American Revolution was fought on that beautiful spring morning, Estabrook fell with a shoulder wounded on Lexington Green from the fire of the British regulars. He might have been the first American to fall in battle during the American Revolution: ironically, a distinction that has been overlooked and forgotten today. Prince Estabrook was one of the forgotten Black who served in the American Revolution, including for years of service in Massachusetts regiments during the course of the

American Revolution, after the initial showdown at Lexington on the most famous April morning in American history.

Ironically, Blacks also engaged in their own civil war, which also has been forgotten. During the struggle for empire in colonial America, officials of the Colony of South Carolina early drafted slaves into the ranks of the militia to defend the vulnerable colony against the threats of not only Native Americans, but also their archenemy to the south, the Catholics of Spanish Florida, whose capital was located at St. Augustine in northeast Florida on the Atlantic coast. But it was the Spanish who first enlisted Blacks, who were mostly escaped slaves from the Colony of South Carolina, and formed them in regular militia companies just like the South Carolinians at a later date. The Spanish bestowed equal rights and citizenship to Blacks on the condition that they became good Catholics, which was eagerly accepted by the former South Carolina slaves who made their dreams come true in St. Augustine. In the same way, so Black Patriots and Black "British" fighting men also engaged in their own civil war during the American Revolution. For instance, Black "British" defenders of the strategic Atlantic port of Savannah, Georgia, meet counterattacking Black Haitians who saved the day for the badly bloodied American-French Army, after it had been repulsed in its suicidal headlong assault on the powerful fortifications that protected Savannah on October 9, 1779.

Of course, both the South Carolinians and Spanish had white officers who commanded Black troops, just like during the colonial period and the American Revolution, which was the same case when the Confederacy first formed its two official Black companies of an infantry battalion at Richmond in early 1865. In this sense, a historical continuum existed between the Black companies formed for the defense of the South during the colonial period, like in the case of South Carolina, and those organized for service to defend the Confederacy in early 1865, because both were created to defend the homeland under severe threat from successive attackers: first Native Americans, then British troops who captured Charles Town in May 1780, and finally invading Union troops, who were determined to crush the life out of the Confederacy in 1865. All in all, these were basically the same motivations of Blacks, both slave and free men, over a period of centuries, which had been long overlooked and forgotten about the Black experience.

In the American Revolution during the desperate days of 1779 when America's fortunes had grown especially dark and the South was about to be invaded by an overpowering British expeditionary force, founding father Alexander Hamilton, a West Indian from the tropical island of St. Croix, and his friend John Laurens, a promising South Carolinian from a wealthy family, both were young lieutenant colonels who served capably on George Washington's staff, advocated for the acceptance of most radical plan of the war: the raising of a Black army to solve the severe manpower problem of not enough white Patriots available in the South to defend South Carolina, when about to be invaded by a mighty British expeditionary force by sea. Even the Continental Congress in Philadelphia endorsed the boldest and most unorthodox plan of the American Revolution, but these politicians in the North decided to allow the individual Southern states to make the final decision in the republican tradition of power to the people in the form of decentralization. However, it was racist Southern politicians, who were mostly wealthy and aristocratic slaveowners, from Georgia and South Carolina who enthusiastically voted the plan down in record time to deprive America of crucial manpower at a critical time, when the infant American nation was facing a severe manpower crisis, especially in the sparsely populated South, when on the verge of not only invasion but also a systematic British conquest, which began with the fall of Charles Town (today's Charleston) in May 1780.

Continuing the tradition of Black participation in America's Second War of Independence, blue-eyed Private William Williams, an escaped Maryland slave of mixed-race who joined the 38th United States Infantry, was one of the few Americans mortally wounded on September 13, 1814, during the British bombardment of Fort McHenry, that guarded the entrance of the harbor of Baltimore, Maryland, when America gained its national anthem penned by Maryland lawyer and slaveowner Francis Scott Key one of the most memorable events during the War of 1812. Although, Private Williams served in one of the most famous battles of the War of 1812, he also has been one of America's forgotten Patriots, including to this day.

And this historical continuum of Black soldiers fighting against America's enemies, especially the more than 200,000 Union soldiers of the United States Colored Troops (USCT), continued unabated in the Civil War, when a large number of Black soldiers fought for the Confederacy, although exact numbers cannot be determined, because of the lack of historical records and documentation but they were certainly much higher than generally thought or imagined. One historian whose views agreed with other respected scholars, Joseph P. Reidy concluded in a scholarly book, entitled *Arming Slaves*, from Yale University Press: "It is likely that one or two hundred thousand free and enslaved men (most of them the latter) provided direct support to Confederate armed forces [in mostly non-combat roles, but also combat roles, and] contributed significantly to the Confederate war effort."

But the best estimate of the experts and historians at prestigious Harvard University today have revealed that between 3,000-6,000 Blacks, both slave and free, fought for the Confederacy as legitimate frighting men, including in the most famous and climactic attack of the Civil War, Pickett's Charge on the final day at Gettysburg, July 3, 1863 and every major battle of the Civil War on both sides of the Mississippi. This fact of large numbers of Black Confederates serving in the ranks was revealed in the words of a shocked Dr. Lewis H. Steiner about General Robert E. Lee's Army of Northern Virginia in the late summer of 1862 during the invasion of Maryland.

He wrote about what he saw at Frederick, nestled in a picturesque setting along the turbid Monocacy River amid the rolling hills of western Maryland, when the Army of Northern Virginia passed through the town during Lee's first invasion of the North: "Most of the Negros [with Lee's Army] had arms, rifles, muskets, sabers, bowie knives, dirks, etc." Clearly, these were fighting men, although they were also slaves like the Helots who fought and died beside King Leonidas and his Spartan warriors at Thermopylae in 480 BC.

Chapter II

The Richmond Government Finally Awakens

Therefore, given the past history of Blacks fighting for America long before the outbreak of the American Revolution, it is not surprising and even unusual when the Confederacy was on the ropes in early 1865 that the time had finally come for the use of Black troops, although too belated to make any difference in the war's overall outcome: a classic case of too little, too late. America's most vocal and articulate Black abolitionist before and during the Civil War, Frederick Douglass early knew and feared as much, writing how: "I am not at all of the opinion of some of the Anti-Slavery press that the slaves of the South will not fight in the interests of the South . . . if Jeff. Davis earnestly goes about the work to raise a black army in the South, making them suitable promises they can be made very effect in a war for Southern independence." Douglass, who had played a key role in raising black troops for the Union, including his two sons who served in the 54th Massachusetts Regiment which was the first Black regiment organized in the North among the free population and won distinction in its famous attack on Fort Wagner, South Carolina, in July 1863, was exactly right in his sage opinion. In addition, Douglass also emphasized how: "If Jeff. Davis will hold out to the blacks of the South their freedom, guarantee their freedom, the possession of a piece of land, and the elective franchise, I should say that the negroes of the South would acting unwisely if they do not fight, and fight valiantly, for this boon," which had been long-awaited by the enslaved people of the South. A former Maryland slave who had escaped to the North, Douglass knew exactly what he was taking about when it came to the feelings and aspirations of black people in bondage.

The Confederate government in Richmond, the nation's beleaguered capital on the James River, finally began to realize that Black soldiers were urgently needed or the Confederacy was doomed. On February 9, 1865, the main African Church and the surrounding area in the capital of Richmond, Virginia, was a beehive of activity marked by a wave of excitement among the population born of sheer desperation and brighter hopes for the future, because of a new idea, since the Confederacy now needed a miracle to survive against the Northern war machine under the North's winningest general, Ulysses S. Grant. Confederate leaders, in a truly desperate situation, were busily rallying members of the capital's Black community, both slave and free, to fight for the Confederacy. Gifted Louisianian Benjamin Judah, who was a leading cabinet member and the most highly-placed Hebrew in the Confederate Government, implored to the large crowd in Richmond in saying words that no one at the capital thought that they would ever hear: "Let us say to every negro who wishes to go into the ranks on the condition of being made free—Go and fight, you are free'." After a lengthy heated debate in the Confederate Congress, this unthinkable and unimaginable reality was about to become official law of the Confederacy.

However, Southern racism in Richmond, especially among the upper class, slave-owning elites, was so strong that resistance to the so-called Black "experiment" continued to be alive and well in early 1865, including in the Confederate Congress at Richmond. In the words of anti-Black Confederate Howell Cobb, a Confederate political general from Georgia where he had served as governor before the war and a former United States Congressman, emphasized how: "The moment your resort to negro soldiers your white soldiers will be lost to you [which was entirely false by 1865] . . . The day you make soldiers of them is the beginning of the end of the revolution. If slaves will make good soldiers our whole theory [of Black inferiority and] slavery is wrong." Ironically, political opposition across the South cried loudly against the use of Black troops especially if freedom was promised to them, while thousands of the white common soldiers in the ranks of General Robert E. Lee's Army of Northern Virginia defending the trenches of Petersburg in 1864-1865 were all for the utilization of Black troops, because they realized that the South was losing a war of attrition and desperately needed manpower to survive.

But the situation on the war front became so desperate with General Grant about to capture strategic Petersburg that the Confederate Congress finally passed the necessary legislation for the use of Black troops on March 13, 1865, thanks in part to the personal endorsement of General Lee, who desperately needed troops for his depleted Army of Northern Virginia that was in the process of dying in this lengthy war of attrition. President Jefferson Davis, thanks partly to General Lee who had emphasized that his hard-pressed troops would welcome Black soldiers in arms to replenish the army's ranks, finally signed his approval on March 13. But more action was needed, because although the Confederate Congress approved Black troops, they refused to free them by adding a manumission clause, considering that controversial act a step much too far. In consequence, Davis made sure that the slaves would become free to ensure higher enlistment and morale in the ranks when he issued his military order for manumission on March 22, which emphasized that the Black soldiers were to be freed for faithful service, circumventing the strong anti-manumission opposition of the Confederate Congress, whose self-serving members would rather see the Confederacy's collapse than bestow freedom to slaves in a rather remarkable and self-defeating development that defied reason in early 1865.

The overall situation of the Confederacy was now desperate, because the Southern nation was now basically in its death throes. At this time and as mentioned, General Ulysses S. Grant was on the verge of capturing the strategic bastion of Petersburg, which supplied Richmond with everything from across the South by rail. And the hard-riding Union cavalrymen of General Phil Sheridan were applying more pressure around Richmond, causing greater alarm in the capital on the James River by destroying railroad lines and outfighting the far weaker Confederate cavalry, which was in bad overall shape in the later stages of the war, falling from its once elevated status of complete superiority. Clearly, drastic action was needed by the reeling Confederacy and now one realized this more than President Davis, which was evident from his military order of March 22 that promised freedom to slaves who fought for the Confederacy and served faithfully in the army's ranks.

Now and most important, Black soldiers, both slave and free men, finally began to enlist in the army and train in Richmond and officially serve in the regular, or national, ranks of the Confederate Army, including shortly in the elaborate network of trenches that surrounded Richmond. The longtime tradition of Blacks serving with Confederate armies in a wide variety of roles, including combat but mostly in vital support roles, helped to set the stage for the official recruitment of Black soldiers by the Confederate Government in what was a relatively smooth and natural transition in the end. This was the first national law for the use of Black troops because of the Confederacy's severe manpower crisis during a long war of attrition by early 1865, which should have been addressed with the use Black Confederates far earlier by the Confederacy to have been effective. Unlike the North that drew new troops from a steady flow of European immigration, especially from Ireland, the South's armies could not replenish their ranks like the Army of the Potomac. As noted and most important, the idea of Black Confederates serving in the army's ranks was enthusiastically supported by the fighting men, including slaveowners, of the manpower-short Army of Northern Virginia, when they had been earlier polled by Confederate officials to get their opinions about this highly sensitive and controversial subject, while they were serving in Petersburg's trenches during the gloomy winter of 1864-1865: a classic race of racism dying in the hope of saving a dying nation.

Again, this concept of Black Confederates in this war was nothing new or novel for the South. In June 1861, Tennessee had been the first Southern state to pass legislation for using free Blacks as fighting men in state service. The other Southern states had also allowed Blacks, both slave and free, to serve the state in helping to repel the invaders of their endangered homeland. Early in the war, quite a few Southern citizens, who were the most enlightened ones, demanded of the Richmond and state governments that the South utilize Black troops, because slaves consisted of such a large percentage of the South's population and these desperate calls only increased with each new Confederate reversal, including the loss of strategic Vicksburg, Mississippi, on the Fourth of July 1862 that won the Mississippi River from the Union and cut the Confederacy in half.

But significantly, since the war's beginning, the Confederate Navy, like the maritime industry and merchant fleet of the South before the war just like in New England, utilized large numbers of Black seamen, both slave and free. Clearly and as noted, in early 1865, the national government at Richmond was extremely belated in its desperate efforts to employ Black Confederate troops, ignoring the wise early 1864 call of the openminded Major General Patrick Ronayne Cleburne, who had born in County Cork, Ireland, to use Black Confederate soldiers to save the day, before it was too late for the beleaguered Confederacy that was slowly but surely losing a brutal war of attrition. Of course, the Richmond government ignored General Cleburne's timely initiative and timely warning of the necessity of employing Black Confederates in organized units in early January 1864. Cleburne's bold proposal for the use of Black Confederate troops basically ensured the ruin of the impressive and distinguished military career of this remarkable Irishman, who was the best division commander in the Army of Tennessee in the entire western theater by 1864. As the most gifted and dynamic upper echelon leader in the Army of Tennessee, Major General Cleburne, age thirty-six, was fated to die in leading the suicidal charge of his troops against a powerful network of Union fortifications in the valley of the Harpeth River at the Battle of Franklin, Tennessee, on November 30, 1864.

At Richmond and with time rapidly running out of the Confederacy's life in early 1865, little additional time had been wasted by the government in creating Black Confederate troops under Majors Thomas P. Turner, who had been the former commandant of Libby Prison, and Joseph W. Pegram. The first Black Confederate soldiers began to train at Smith's Factory that was located at Main and Twenty-first Street in Richmond. The astounding news of Black Confederate training in the nation's capital appeared in the pages of the *Sentinel* of Richmond on March 21, 1865 and caused a sensation throughout the capital city: "the company of colored troops [in uniform] will parade on the [main] square [of the capitol] on Wednesday evening . . . This is the first company of negro troops raised in Virginia." This first company was shortly increased to two battalions, which initially included Black men, both slave and free, recruited from the Army of Northern Virginia and the large military hospitals at Camp Winder and Camp Jackson. As mentioned, these fast-paced developments caused "quite a sensation" in Richmond, because so many white citizens were in utter disbelief.

And as revealed in a *Richmond Daily Dispatch* article: "Parade.—Yesterday afternoon [two Black Confederate companies were] paraded on the Capitol Square" in Richmond [and in the infantry battalion] were two companies of negroes, which were made up from the negroes employed about the hospitals . . . In marked contrast to the appearance of these negroes was that of a squad of Major [Thomas P.] Turner's colored troops, neatly uniformed, and showing a good soldierly carriage [and the] Volunteering [of additional Black soldiers] would be much encouraged by the parade of Majors Pegram's and Turner's men, which will, we hope, soon take place."

All Richmond seemed to have turned out to watch the Confederacy's newest fighting men of a darker due, because such a remarkable development was only recently thought unimaginable, especially in the nation's capital. Significantly and as noted, an unknown number of free Blacks of Richmond had also joined the new infantry battalion of mostly slaves in the desire to defend their native homeland, just like the white soldiers with Southern nationalism in the air, when the Yankees were so close to Richmond and about to squeeze the life out of Petersburg. On March 25, 1865, the *Richmond Enquirer* described the unbelievable sight: "The appearance of the battalion of colored troops in the Square [dominated by the large equestrian statue of George Washington] attracted thousands of our citizens [who were] all eager to glimpse the sable soldiers. The [military] bearing of the negroes elicited universal commendation [and] they went through the manual of arms in a manner which would have done credit to veteran soldiers, while the evolutions of the line were executed with promptness and precision. As an appropriate recognition of their promptness in forming the first battalion of colored troops in the Confederacy, we suggest to the [white] ladies of Richmond the propriety of presenting the battalion with an appropriate banner," like in the case of white Confederate units in which the soldiers prized nothing more than their flags, while often dying to preserve them in the heat of battle and keep these precious banners out of Yankee hands.

After intense training and the instilling of proper soldierly discipline, the Black Confederates, both slave and free, were sent to man positions in the sprawling defenses of Richmond. General Lee's views, which revealed the wisdom and fairmindedness for which he was so well-known, about the importance of Black troops and how to ensure their faithful service were emphasized by his most reliable staff officer Lieutenant Colonel Charles Marshall, who had been born in Virginia and a family friend of the Lee family before the war: "the negroes should know that the service is voluntary. As to the name of the troops, the general thanks you cannot do better than consult the [Black] men themselves . . . Everything should be done to impress them with the responsibility and character of their position [and] they should be treated to feel that their obligations are those of any other soldier and their rights and privileges dependent in law & order as obligations upon others as upon themselves. Harshness and contemptuous or offensive language or conduct to them must be forbidden and they should be made to forget as soon as possible that they are regarded as menials."

In the end, "several hundred [Black men, both free and slave] had been uniformed and smaller numbers drilled and trained" in Richmond for service in the trenches of Richmond to oppose the ominous threat of Army of the Potomac. Fortunately, the Black Confederates were made better soldiers by the tireless efforts of two excellent young officers of merit, Majors Joseph W. Pegram and Thomas P. Turner. As revealed in the pages of the *Daily Dispatch* of Richmond on March 16, 1865: "We understand that to Major J. W. Pegram and Major T. P. Turner have been assigned the duty of organizing and training the negro soldiers, preparatory to putting them in the field. They are both young officers of the highest promise, distinguished alike for gallantry in the field and for skill in their discharge of this peculiar duty.—They speak in the most encouraging terms of the enterprise, both expressing the belief that the negro under proper officers will make an excellent soldier."

Then, the editor made a key point that might have saved the Confederacy from a slow, agonizing death, but it was now too late having missed out on a golden opportunity: "It is a great pity this had not been done six months ago. But we may yet derive enormous benefit from the experiment's success to these gallant young officers." Considerable progress was made throughout March and even into early April when the pleasant spring weather was growing warmer in central Virginia. Then, on March 27, an article in the *Richmond Examiner* described how the Black Confederate troops "are drilled by daily for several hours by Lieutenant Virginus Bossieux [of French descent], whose talent peculiarly adapts him to imparting instructions in the manual. About a dozen of the recruits are free negroes, who have enlisted on their own free will and choice [to shatter the myth of simply slave soldiers serving in the ranks of the Black infantry battalion]. Recruits are coming in [daily and their drill has revealed] something remarkable. They moved with evident pride and satisfaction to themselves . . . Major Turner hopes to recruit and equip a command [company] of eighty or a hundred in a few weeks . . . Meanwhile the owners of slaves have a duty to perform in sending forward recruits and infusing them a spirity emulation among the negroes. Let all hands go to work with energy."

The *Richmond Examiner* printed another revealing article on April 3, 1865 entitled, *The Battalion*: "The work of recruiting negroes for the Confederate States army goes on bravely at the rendezvous of Major Pegram and Turner, corner of Cary and Twenty first, and those skeptics who doubt the availability of negroes as soldiers immediately would be established in the faith of the opposite doctrine by a visit to the rendezvous where the battalion is drilled daily. We may not state numbers, but the several organizations are filling up with a gratifying rapidity." What was especially noteworthy and significant, as reported the *Richmond Examiner*, was the fact that the "free negroes who have enlisted on their own free will and choice."

The exact numbers of the Confederacy's first and only official Black troops has been debated to this day, but at least initially the infantry battalion of two companies consisted of "about two hundred," perhaps even more and as many as 300 fighting men, in the words of one Southerner. As mentioned, some of the first Black soldiers, both slaves and free men, were hastily dispatched to defend the works that protected Richmond, because of the severe shortage of manpower and with overpowering numbers of

Federals capable of launching massive assaults at any moment. The *Evening Star* of Washington, D.C., on March 30, carried the story how a "deserter from the rebel army . . . reports that rebel authorities have already placed a number of negro troops in the entrenchments surrounding Richmond," which were desperately short of manpower from both the ravages of a brutal attrition and mass desertions that had occurred throughout the miserable winter of 1864-1865.

Chapter III

Fast-Paced Strategic Developments

Now commanding the Army of the Potomac that was slowing squeezing the life out of Petersburg to force its eventual fall which would then cause Richmond likewise to fall like a domino, General Ulysses S. Grant was the most remarkable military man produced during the Civil War. At least initially, he seemed not to have been made to be a soldier, however. Just out of the United States Military Academy at West Point, New York, young Grant had entered the Mexican-American War as a freshly-minted lieutenant, who detested the injustice of America's war against the politically-torn and impoverished Republic of Mexico from 1846-1848. He had correctly seen the larger United States of having been guilty of a great national sin: taking advantage of its weaker and politically divided neighbor in what was nothing more than a giant land grab by an aggressive and imperialistic United States in which the Republic of Mexico would lose half of its territory in the end, the Southwest and including California, which was a primary goal of expansionist President James K. Polk.

For as long as he could remember, Grant loved horses not war, especially the imperialistic conflict with a hapless Mexico. Grant was so young, quiet, feminine-looking, and shy that he played the part of a woman in soldier's play, while in a tented camp along the Nueces River in south Texas and the southernmost river in Texas north of the Rio Grande, when General Zackary Taylor's little army was preparing for the march south to the Rio Grande River, which was deep in territory of the Republic of Mexico. Despite hating the war, Grant won distinction for courage and in performing well beyond the call of duty, excelling as a young officer in his first combat and performing like a season veteran. Grant was a natural soldier and a very good one.

However, Grant's personal fortunes sank after his glory days in the Mexican-American War 1846-1848. Disillusioned and saddled with the reputation of having a drinking problem at remote outposts in the West during misery assignments since he was unhappy in missing his wife and family, he retired from the United States Army in 1854. But despite having failed in numerous occupations before the Civil War and enduring a frustrating life except for a happy marriage to Julia Dent, Grant early emerged in the western theater as President Abraham Lincoln's most aggressive and capable general with a distinct penchant for winning unlike any other Union commander. This lover of horses who detested the sight of blood won battles and conquered enemy armies across the western theater with regularly and seemingly with relative ease, beginning with his capture of strategic Forts Henry and Donelson, which opened up the upper South in the region east of the Mississippi to Union invasions, in early 1862. Grant then captured the strategic bastion of Vicksburg, Mississippi, on the mighty Mississippi River, which surrendered to him on the Fourth of July 1863. For these victories that turned the tide of war in the West in the Union's favor, Grant steadily rose to the top until he won command of the Army of the Potomac. He then brilliantly orchestrated the spring 1864 Campaign in Virginia which would become known as the Overland Campaign, in a bid to capture Richmond, heralding the end of the Confederacy in April 1865. The resourceful and relentless Grant became President Lincoln's best and most trustworthy general and these two westerners and friends became the dynamic and talented leadership team that eventually won the Civil War for the Union.

During the bloodiest campaign of the Civil War in 1864, Grant steadily pushed south and ever closer to Richmond, refusing to retreat despite suffering high losses which was the usual case with the often-defeated Army of the Potomac, especially after the Battles of the Wilderness and then after Grant's suicidal assaults against Lee's strong fortifications at Cold Harbor, Virginia. At that time, the Army of the Potomac lost a stagging 11,000 men on the killing fields of Cold Harbor just northeast of Richmond, but Grant remained undaunted. He had failed in his gamble to destroy Lee's Army and drive it into the Richmond defenses at a frightful cost in lives, but he was motivated to end the war as soon as possible, which inevitably meant a high loss of life. To avoid other such slaughters of his troops because Richmond was defended so tenaciously and the South had its most gifted commander leading the Army of Northern Virginia, General Lee, Grant then made a bold decision to target Petersburg, Virginia, just south of the capital, because it was a railroad hub and supply center that had long funneled manpower and supplies north to Richmond. Capturing Petersburg equated to capturing Richmond, which was fully appreciated by General Grant. This required a stealthy movement by Grant south to catch Lee by surprise with a fast-moving Army of the Potomac crossing the James River, which flowed through Richmond, on a giant ponton train. Grant then headed south for Petersburg, which was ill-prepared for a stout defense of the vital city on the Appomattox River.

Narrowly missing the opportunity of capturing a lightly defended defenses, only men and boys of the local militia held the earthworks, of Petersburg in mid-June by the bungling of his generals after having successfully crossed to the south side of the James River, Grant settled into the long siege of Petersburg. Both sides built massive fortifications reminiscent of the western front during the First World War. As Grant planned in what would become the longest siege in American history, the capture of the vital railroad center on the muddy Appomattox River would force the evacuation of Richmond, which would then be completely cut off. Increasing Grant's already high chances for success, General Sheridan had already joined him south of the James River near the end of March 1865 to add muscle and a quick strike force to the Army of the Potomac and expanding its size to more than 120,000 troops, including a large number of Black Union troops of the USCT. Because of the vastly superior manpower advantage and with the capable General Sheridan, whose possessed aggressive top lieutenants like General George Armstrong Custer, able to cut railroad lines, Grant could maneuver at will to eventually force Lee out of strategic Petersburg that served as the vital lifeline for Richmond just to the north.

For such reasons, General Lee knew that Petersburg could not be held with his weak hand of too few men, or about half the number of Grant's troops, especially when Grant continued to move to the left to outflank Confederate positions and cut railroad lines with both infantry and cavalry. Knowing that the worst case scenario was drawing near and accepting the inevitable, Lee wrote to the Confederate government on February 8, 1865 and emphasized how: "You must not be surprised if calamity befalls us." That calamity began in earnest when Confederate troops under General George E. Pickett were routed on April 1 at Five Forks, Virginia, located just southwest of Petersburg, which was the breaking point for the Army of Northern Virginia that lost around 7,000 men which it could ill-afford to lose in an unprecedented disaster, while the strategic South Side Railroad, which had long supplied the men of Petersburg, was severed by the Yankees. The fortunes of war had decidedly turned against the Army of Northern Virginia and the Confederacy, which was the much-dreaded dawn of its darkest hour.

Holding all the tactical high cards, General Grant knew that it was time to deliver an overpowering blow and it was time to capture Petersburg, ordering a massive infantry assault on April 2. The successful assault broke the siege and all but cut Lee's Army in half. With Lee's last supply line severed and badly outnumbered and low on everything, he had no choice but to order the evacuation of Petersburg, which guaranteed the evacuation and loss of Richmond, the nation's capital. Now caught in his most desperate situation, Lee planned to withdraw all his forces west from both Petersburg and Richmond and concentrate them in the picturesque piedmont of central Virginia at Amelia Court House, Virginia, which was located slightly northwest of Petersburg and about thirty-six miles and about forty miles southwest of Richmond: roughly a half-way point on the dreary Confederate retreat west. Lee hoped to gain the Richmond and Danville Railroad because of its vital links to General Joseph Johnston's Army of Tennessee now in northern North Carolina. General Lee's only hope was now to link the Army of Tennessee with what little was left of the Army of Northern Virginia, so that the resistance effort could be continued for the preservation of the Confederacy's life.

Meanwhile, Grant made plans to launch an all-out assault on Petersburg to break the last lines of resistance on the early morning of April 3, but it proved unnecessary. He entered the deserted city on the Appomattox River, but it was too late by then because the Confederates had evacuated. A humane man, Grant could have ordered his artillery to fire at the retreating Rebel column moving at a slow rate out of the western end of Petersburg, but he decided otherwise almost out of pity, because the end of the Confederacy was so near and he knew that they were bound to be captured. The Confederates had retreated west from Petersburg in the darkness of April 2 and narrowly escaped getting cutoff by the fast-moving Army of the Potomac. Richmond was evacuated at the same time because the capital was now doomed with Petersburg's loss. President Davis and his cabinet, including Judah Benjamin, departed on a train of the Richmond & Danville Railroad just before midnight on April 2 and headed for Danville, Virginia, which was located just north of the North Carolina border and southwest of Richmond. The scene in Richmond was one of complete panic and chaos. Supply depots were burned because they could not be evacuated in time to keep them out of Yankee hands. Grant ordered his troops to pursue west along the south side of the Appomattox River for the "purpose of heading off Lee," in Grant words of determination that were the watchwords for achieving decisive victory in early April 1865. General Grant ordered his troops "to get ahead of him and cut him off" to end the Army of Northern Virginia's life, if everything went according to plan.

Meanwhile, the Black Confederate troops of the two companies of a full infantry battalion had been ordered to play a key role, serving as escorts and guardians of the main and last supply wagon train, which included rations, baggage, and munitions, out of Richmond, before everything had gone up in flames which eventually was the case before arriving Union troops put out the fires, including an endangered large black powder magazines before they exploded. In the lengthy column of the last rebel reserves of General Custis Lee, the long wagon train, driven by black and white teamsters and which was invaluable for Lee's supply-short retreating army, had already moved out from Richmond, heading southwest for Amelia Court House, where Lee and the Army of Northern Virginia hoped to unite as one in a final concentration of the badly depleted rebel army that had been racked by desertions throughout the winter and spring. All the while, Grant was pushing his forces rapidly west to intercept and cutoff Lee's Army, while hoping to deliver a killing blow from which the Army of Northern Virginia would never recover.

Since General Lee was sorely disappointed, if not angered, by the non-arrival of supplies at Amelia Court House by train, he still possessed the possibility that the main supply train, guarded by the Black Confederate soldiers, might still reach his famished men in time. His level of frustration had reached new heights, because miscommunications had resulted when the eager Confederates finally opened the doors of the long line of railroad boxcars at Amelia Court House Station to find that nothing had been sent, when they had expected to find the 300,000 rations that he had been ordered from Richmond.

This stunning logistical setback was one of the greatest self-inflicted wounds in the history of the Confederacy that was additionally doomed with each new grievous mistake made by the Confederates in the confusion of evacuation and retreat west, where the Confederates hoped safety could be found.

After crossing to the south side of the Appomattox River, the wagon train from Richmond with General Custis Lee's column was located just north of Amelia Court House on April 4, while Lee's Army continued to come together and regroup at Amelia Court House, before it was too late. Lee had specially ordered the long train of wagons from the capital to take the route through Painesville, located just northwest of Amelia Court House, and then to join the gathering army at Amelia Court House. Now, on April 4, Lee was forced to rely on his meager reserve rations that had come by the wagons of forging details sent into the countryside, but they came back largely empty of provisions of any kind on the morning of April 5: hence, the importance of the main wagon train of supplies from Richmond and now guarded by the Black Confederates in an increasingly crucial role.

Even more, the long delay—a fatal one because of the race of both armies west--in waiting in vain for rations and the arrival of troops from Richmond and Petersburg at Amelia Court House hour after hour on April 4 had cost General Lee precious time of a full day, which allowed the Federal cavalry to not only overtake the weary Rebels but also to eventually get ahead of their line of westward retreat to Danville, when General Lee desperately needed all the extra time that he could get for his proposed attempt to reach General Joseph E. Johnston and the Army of Tennessee to the south in northern North Carolina. But Johnston had already been defeated by General William T. Sherman's Army of Tennessee at Bentonville, North Carolina, on March 19-21, leaving the Army of Northern Virginia on its own.

In a fatal development and as noted, General Lee had lost his precious lead on Grant's relentless pursuers, and it would never be regained by him. Additionally sealing the fate of the reeling Army of Northern Virginia was the feat performed by the advance of General Phil Sheridan's troopers, when they reached Jetersville, which was located on the Richmond & Danville Railroad just south of Painesville and southwest of Amelia Court House and on the route to Danville, on the evening of April 4 and bluecoat troopers entered the telegraph office. Here, they intercepted Lee's all-important telegraphic message that was about to be sent to the Confederate Commissary Department, requesting 200,000 rations to be sent to Danville, which Lee expected to reach in his continued retreat to the southwest. This overall disastrous situation revealed the great importance of the main supply train, which contained at least 20,000 rations from Richmond, guarded by the infantry battalion of Black Confederate troops of around 200 men, or even more, who had been entrusted with the wagon train's safety since departing Richmond.

Ironically, one of the key players who had trained and disciplined the two battalions of Black troops was not with the last wagon train from Richmond that was now moving with General Custis Lee's long column of retreating troops, which was attempting to reach Amelia Court House, where Lee was concentrating his forces from Richmond and Petersburg, Major Thomas P. Turner.

Turner's letter, as reprinted in the July 17, 1895 issue of the *New York Times*, revealed his situation in the confusion of a chaotic evacuation of Richmond and retreat at night: "On the 3rd of April last, I left Richmond; it was the day on which the Yankees entered . . . On reaching Gen. Lee's army, I found everything in chaos and confusion; the roads and avenues were filled with fugitives, hurrying on God knows were."

Major Turner was unable to find his command of Black Confederates, who he had trained and disciplined in Richmond along with Major Joseph W. Pegram.

In consequence, Turner was destined not to fight at Painesville in western Amelia County, Virginia, on the morning of April 5 unlike Major Pegram, who now commanded the newly raised infantry battalion of Black Confederates, both slaves eager to win their freedom and free blacks who were eager to demonstrate their combat prowess, on their long journey southwest to Painesville and a rendezvous with destiny in the first week of April in the Virginia Piedmont.

Final Showdown Near Painesville,
April 5, 1865

Meanwhile, the entire Army of the Potomac was consumed with a level of hectic activity that had not been previously seen in a most aggressive pursuit, because the Federals knew that the end of the Army of Northern Virginia was drawing ever closer in this Virginia springtime of decision, when so much was at stake for America. From Confederate prisoners, the troopers of the 1st New Jersey Cavalry Regiment learned that General Lee was desperately attempting to form his army at Amelia Court House, which he, as noted, had entered in the hope of securing the 200,000 rations that he had ordered from the Confederate Commissary Department, but they never arrived by rail from Richmond to the shock of the commander-in-chief. By 3:00 am on April 5, the entire cavalry brigade of Brigadier General Henry E. Davies, as ordered by division commander General George Crook who had been directed to do so by Sheridan who had become suspicious why that the ever-aggressive Lee was not attacking and, hence, might be attempting to slip around him, was on the move. This fine brigade of veteran horse soldiers consisted of the 1st New Jersey, 10th New York, 24th New York, and five companies of the 1st Pennsylvania Cavalry and an experienced artillery battery, Battery A, the 2nd United States Artillery: all part of Major General George Crook's 2nd Cavalry Division, Army of the

Potomac. At this time, Crook ordered Davies, who rode out from Jetersville, to reconnoiter his left flank and front to determine what Lee was up to since he was well-known for his craftiness and elusiveness. However, General Lee was still at Amelia Court House where his forces were yet gathering, after the lengthy withdrawals from both Petersburg and Richmond.

Meanwhile, trusty rebel scouts had informed the commander of the Black Confederates troops, Major Joseph W. Pegram, that Yankee cavalry was on the way along the main road leading directly toward them. Here, about four miles outside the town of Painesville and as ordered by Major Pegram, the Black Confederates stacked their Enfield muskets in neat rows, as they had been trained to do. On Major Pegram's orders, they immediately began to construct a light earthwork as directed by Confederate engineers to take advantage of good natural setting and defensive ground to protect the wagon train that had come to a halt, including the hectic gathering fence rails to place on top of the earthen parapet. Believing that they were legitimate fighting men after around three weeks of intense training in Richmond and now with their Enfield rifles stacked in neat rows not far from the light breastworks, the Black Confederates were disgruntled that they had been ordered to do menial work like slaves instead of fighting like men: a partial indication of high morale and a esprit de corps of the infantry battalion of Black Confederates. Nevertheless, they worked frantically, knowing that it was only a matter of time before the Federals appeared in large numbers to attack the precious wagon train so badly needed by General Lee. Arriving in the small town of Painesville at the head of his cavalrymen, General Davies learned that an immense Confederate wagon train was located nearby, moving in the direction of Ameila Court House. He immediately led his cavalry brigade in frantic pursuit. As mentioned, the Black Confederates held the most advanced and foremost earthwork protecting the wagons without the presence white soldiers of General Custis Lee's command. In protective fashion, the ebony fighting men now represented the first line of defense just before the long line of supply wagons strewn out along the road just behind them.

All of a sudden, the lengthy blue line of the 1st New Jersey Volunteer Cavalry hurriedly formed atop an open elevation on the horizon that overlooked the main road and the long line of Confederate wagons, nestled on the lower ground of a slight valley through which the main road ran, seemingly at their mercy. After having quickly formed for action behind the light earthworks that protected the 180 supply wagons to the beating of drums of Black drummer boys and Major Pegram's shouted orders, the Black Confederate soldiers, both slaves and free men, must have been astonished by the sight of the gathering formations of New Jersey troopers situated above them on the high ground that dominated this picturesque area of the Virginia Piedmont in western Amelia County, but not one of the Black infantry battalion lost their nerve at this anxiety-filled moment.

Around 10:00 am, the blaring of brass bugles prepared the veteran New Jersey troopers for the attack, while they aligned in neat rows for the unleashing of a sweeping cavalry charge straight downhill and over a grassy field leading to the road full of wagons. To Yankee eyes, the target situated below them could not have been more inviting and tantalizing—the prize of a lengthy train of so many vulnerable wagons overflowing with supplies, especially precious rations that were the last foodstuffs that still had a chance of reaching the Army of Northern Virginia at Amelia Court House, after the railroad train from the Commissary Department in Richmond had failed to deliver rations as ordered by General Lee. Therefore and as mentioned, this wagon train now protected by the Black Confederates just northwest of Amelia Court House was crucial for the maintaining of the life of Lee's Army, which most of all needed rations to feed the starving and weary men in the weary ranks of gray and butternut.

But the New Jersey troopers of this fine cavalry regiment did not know this crucial piece of information because it did not matter to them, because they had been ordered to attack the enemy at first sight. Quite simply and most significant, this final supply wagon out of Richmond represented the last and only rations for the Army of Northern Virginia, which would not survive much longer without rations or supplies. In consequence, what was about to happen in this western part of Amelia County, Virginia, near the small town of Painesville, or Paines Cross Roads as it was locally known, was extremely important given the overall desperate strategic situation of not only Lee's Army, but also the Confederacy at this crucial time of supreme crisis.

Meanwhile, Colonel Hugh Hartshorne Janeway, who commanded the hundreds of troopers of the 1st New Jersey Cavalry at only age twenty-two, was a remarkable and highly capable young officer. He had been promoted to the lofty rank of colonel in October 1864. He commanded a fine, veteran regiment that had been organized at Trenton, New Jersey, where George Washington had won his miracle victory over a full brigade of Hessians of three disciplined and well-trained German regiments on the early snowy morning of December 26, 1776 to save the dying revolution, in August 1861. The New Jersey regiment had fought with distinction during the largest cavalry battle of the Civil War at Brandy Station, Virginia, on June 9, 1863, and then in the campaign that resulted in the three awful days of bloodletting at Gettysburg, Pennsylvania, in early July 1863. Janeway was destined to survive the Battle of Painesville on the morning of April 5 about two hours before noon, but he would be shot in the head and killed instantly in leading the charge at Amelia Springs, just southeast of Painesville, later in the day on April 5. All in all, April 5 was destined to be a sad day for the 1st New Jersey Cavalry in its distinguished history.

Meanwhile, with cocked Enfield rifles, around 200, or more, Black Confederates in new gray uniforms were ready and waiting behind the light earthworks, while under the capable leadership of Major Pegram. The upcoming cavalry attack of the New Jersey regiment had to be thwarted at all costs, because this supply train was invaluable and must be preserved since it was the last one that had left Richmond before it had fallen to the victorious Yankees. Here, in the light breastwork aligned beside the dirt road to protect the long line of supply wagons, the Black Confederate soldiers made their last stand on the morning of April 5. The hasty erecting of the light defenses by digging a shallow ditch and throwing up earth for the creation of a parapet, strengthened by fence rails, across the open ground by the Black Confederates was certainly a wise decision with the troopers of the 1st New Jersey Cavalry now about to attack. With Lee's Army at Amelia Court House just to the southeast starving because of the lack of rations and as mentioned, it was absolutely crucial for the Black Confederate to hold firm and protect the precious wagons full of invaluable foodstuffs now so badly needed by what was left of the once-invincible Army of Northern Virginia in its glory days of 1862.

With the sharp notes of brass bugles blaring through the warm air of April 5, the lengthy line of New Jersey horsemen on the high ground poured down the grassy slope with sabers flashing in the early spring sunlight. The sight of the imposing cavalry charge—the first ever seen by the Black Confederates of a full infantry battalion of two companies, under the capable Major Pegram, who were in their first action—was an impressive one, while the rookie ebony fighting men watched in silence with cocked Enfield rifles, caliber .577, that had been imported all the way from

England. Ironically, the Black Confederates were now armed with an excellent firearm that was superior to those used by many white Southern soldiers and Union soldiers. And wearing new Confederate uniforms of gray, they were also better clothed than the vast majority of veteran soldiers, or old campaigners, of not only their own army but also of the Army of the Potomac at this time.

Here, about four miles outside the small town of Painesville just northwest of Amelia Court House, the full battalion of slaves and free Blacks, with leather cartridge-boxes full of forty paper cartridges at their sides, made ready for their greatest challenge during their first and last battle of the Civil War for them. Fortunately, Major Pegram now had his men fully prepared for action to meet the upcoming charge by the 1st New Jersey Cavalry. Hardly before the ebony troops had even aligned along the earthworks topped with fence rails, a tide of Federal cavalry swarmed down the hill in a thundering charge and descended toward the Black Confederates with fast-firing revolvers and carbines blazing, while colorful, silk battle-flags of the New Jersey boys waved in the air. The moment of truth had finally come for the Black Confederates, and nobody knew what would happen next. Would they fight or run? No one knew the answer to this key question at this time, not even these men of African heritage or, of course, Major Pegram. In this war, few rookie white troops on either side in their first battle had stood firm in the face of a sweeping cavalry charge, which was especially the case in 1861.

Fortunately, for the novice Black Confederates, they possessed excellent white officers, especially Major Pegram who had a sufficient amount of experience and knew exactly how to command young soldiers in such a key battlefield situation and they provided excellent leadership to the rookie ebony soldiers. Most important, these white officers had treated these men of African descent fairly and decently as General Lee, who always seemed to know what was best, had specifically ordered. Because the long wagon train, which contained an estimated 20,000 rations, was vital to the continued existence of what was left of the Army of Northern Virginia, the white leaders of these Black defenders were not about to make the common mistake in such a situation of so many infantry officers in facing a full-blown and sweeping cavalry charge pouring down a hill straight toward the defenders: ordering their men to fire too soon to commit the folly of unleashing a premature volley and at too long a range for the first fire to prove effective against the hard-charging cavalrymen, ensuring that the shots would go too high and miss their bluecoat targets.

Instead, Major Pegram, who was in charge of the battalion of Black troops in the absence of Major Turner, calmly waited for exactly the right time to give the order to fire, allowing hundreds of charging New Jersey troopers to get ever closer to their intended victims. Standing or crouched behind the light earthwork and earthen parapet lined with fence rails before the lengthy row of wagons, the Black Confederates grew tense and nervous for what seemed like an eternity to them, while awaiting the order from Major Pegram to open fire. Finally, the dramatic moment came at last and the experienced Confederate major finally ordered "Fire!." A sheet of flame erupted from the row of muskets of the Black Confederates, when the New Jersy cavalrymen were at close range. Major Pegram had ordered his ebony men to open fire at exactly the right time.

A hail of bullets swept through the ranks of the charging cavalry regiment. New Jersey troopers toppled off their horses and the attack immediately fell into disarray. Most important, the momentum of the cavalry attack was broken by the accurate volley unleashed by the Black Confederates at close range. A frustrated Colonel Janeway had no choice but to order his hard-hit men to retreat back up the grassy slope to the open hilltop with the repulse of his cavalry charge that had seemed as if nothing could stop it in the beginning. General Davies then brought up the rest of this brigade and ordered a charge, which included the reformed 1st New Jersey Cavalry Regiment, despite having been bloodied by the Black Confederates.

With a great cheer, thousands of Yankee cavalrymen swarmed over the light earthen defenses, where most of the Black Confederates, who now faced odds that were simply too great, surrendered at the defenses, when surrounded by bluecoat troopers.

Then, the battle grew in scale when the cavalry attackers struck the Confederates of Custis Lee's command and dispersed them, capturing large numbers of prisoners, five battle-flags (it is now known but almost certainly one or two of these silk banners might well have been those of the two companies of the infantry battalion of Black Confederates, especially if each company possessed a flag), and some artillery.

Major Pegram was captured at the head of his Black battalion, having done his duty to the very end and having performed with valor and extremely well just like his Black Confederates, who had now become captives.

The 180 captured wagons of General Custis Lee's column were then destroyed and burned by troopers of the 1st Pennsylvania Cavalry, which had been organized at Harrisburg, Pennsylvania, in August 1861 and fought at Brandy Station, and the 24th New York Cavalry, after General Davies had ordered the troopers to ride the length of the wagon train to capture it and wipe out the last resistance.

In total, 310 Blacks, including teamsters, were taken prisoner along with 320 whites in this debacle for Confederate arms. Significantly, the number of Blacks captured at the Battle of Painesville was nearly equal to the number of white prisoners in these desperate times, when white and Black Confederates had fought together under the same flag.

Almost certainly, an unknown number of other Black Confederates escaped during the confusion and chaos of battle, but this total, evidently fairly high of perhaps around 100 men at most, has never been documented.

All in all, the fighting near Painesville did not last long compared to most other battles, because the action was fast and furious and the war was nearly over.

In the words of Private R. D. Boswell, Confederate Signal Corps, who watched the swirling combat over possession of the wagon train: "I observed some Union Cavalry [1st New Jersey] a short distance away on elevated [open] ground forming to charge and the negro soldiers forming to meet the attack, that was met successfully, the Union regiment retreating [and then] they charged again and the negro troops surrendered," almost certainly on Major Pegram's orders, because this was clearly a no-win situation and he desired not to see his ebony men needlessly slaughtered for nothing by seemingly too many Yankees to count. Interestingly, the official 1st New Jersey Cavalry report of the battle, written on May 25, 1865 by Major Walter R. Robbins, failed to mention any Black Confederates, which helped to obscure their role at the Battle of Painesville, evidently because he considered it no honor at all for his regiment to fight Black Confederates, which was a common white sentiment of the day.

When General Lee learned of the disaster near Painesville and loss of his son's supply train northwest of Amelia Court House, he dispatched his own hard-riding cavalry to chastise the hard-hitting Federal cavalrymen, but it was already too late and all that remained at the site of the battle, which was one of the last engagements of the Civil War, were the long row of burned wagons.

Most important, the Union victory near Painesville emboldened General Phil Sheridan, of Irish descent, who wrote the following glowing dispatch to General Grant on April 5: "General Davies, whom I sent to Painesville on their right flank, has just captured six pieces of artillery and some wagons—We can capture the Army of Northern Virginia if force enough can be thrown to this point, and then advance upon it . . . General Lee is a Amelia Court House in person. They are out of rations, or nearly so . . . ."

Epilogue

The Civil War finally sputtered to an end only four days after the Battle of Painesville, when General Lee and the collapsing Army of Northern Virginia was forced to surrender to General Grant at Appomattox Court House, Virginia, on Palm Sunday, April 9, 1865, when Union troops, both cavalry and infantry, had aligned before, or west, of what little was left of Lee's Army to block the retreat west, winning the desperate race west. Other Black Confederates fought in little known actions, or mere skirmishes, besides the Battle of Painesville on April 5, 1865. Private James Miles, 185th New York Volunteer Infantry, penned in his diary in early 1865 how the "sergt said the war is close to being over [because he saw] several negros [sic] fighting for those rebels." But as noted, the largest group of organized Black Confederates, consisting of around 200 men or more, were those soldiers who fought at the Battle of Painesville on the fateful morning of April 5. A chaplain of a Pennsylvania regiment wrote in triumph how: "The first installment of Rebel prisoners, numbering seventeen hundred and seventy, have just passed, under a special guard . . . In the squad were many negroes recently armed by Jeff. Davis."

But, in the end, it was all too little, too late, when the Confederate Congress had finally authorized Black troops on March 13, 1865, after a great deal of heated debate. For this bold plan of utilizing large numbers of Black soldiers to fight for the Confederacy to have any realistic chance of working as optimistically envisioned in Richmond, then it should have been early adopted in early January 1864, at the latest, when Major General Patrick R. Cleburne, a real fighting man who had been born in Ireland and who was less prejudiced than most Southerners, made the incredibly bold proposal for the use of Black Confederates that was thoroughly rejected by his fellow high-ranking generals of the Army of Tennessee: in the end, a decision that helped to seal the dismal fate of the Confederacy, because there was no other way that the South could have possibly won a lengthy war of attrition against a far more numerous and powerful opponent than without large numbers of Black Confederates called into service at an early date, even before 1864.

Joseph Goebbels, who was Adolf Hitler's brilliantly evil and sinister head of the Nazi Propaganda Office, would almost certainly have been smiling from his grave at the newest "Big Lie" in American history. Today, political agendas have led to the rewriting of history to create a new myth along the lines of a liberal political agenda and to dismiss key contributions to Southern history and a significant chapter in the Black experience, which was all about the courage and sacrifice of large numbers of Black Confederates, including at the Battle of Painesville. As all experienced propagandists know, the most effective way to influence others is to tell the biggest lie because it will still be believed if repeated enough. Best of all, why not place the "Big Lie" in the title of a book? To Levin's credit, the title of *Searching for Black Confederates* was actually quite brilliant in a Machiavellian and commercial sense, because it has incorrectly emphasized that evidence of Black Confederates is so rare and virtually non-existent that a great search had to be conducted that much have been extremely exhausting, both mentally and physically, in the end.

Of course and as revealed in full in my two books, one in 2018 and this current book in 2023, about Black Confederates, this is absolute complete nonsense and hogwash to fool the public that is more gullible than ever before because of the propagandizing of political correctness and corrupt liberal politicians and a lying government, especially in the festering cesspool of Washington, D.C. Even a brief routine search of Google or Civil War primary and secondary documents, including both Northern and Southern newspapers, including even the *New York Times and New York Herald*, has revealed that the sizeable existence of Black Confederate fighting men. The creation of a modern myth based on popular liberal political thought and agendas that are fashionable today with the political Left in America and the dictates of political correctness has been certainly a sad commentary. Perhaps Mr. Levin should secure a GoFundMe internet site to recover some of the great expenses and costs that he must have expended in his epic and exhaustive search of Black

Confederates that must have taken many years, if not an entire lifetime, based on the title of his book?

Levin has employed some of the comparable misleading and history-distorting tactics of David Irving, who is a notorious Holocaust denier, and this British citizen's twisted and perverse views could not be more wrong-headed and on the wrong side of history that have rightly made him infamous around the world. Mr. Levin is a Black Confederate fighting man denier, despite the ample amount of historical evidence that has revealed otherwise. Like in Socialist and Communist countries that have long brainwashed their citizens by rewriting history, some of these same kind of strategies of denying historical facts have been often seen in today's corrupt politics at the national level, when American politicians, including presidents, will say and do practically anything to fool the people in their attempts to prompt their political agendas and get reelected at any cost, especially at the glaring expense of the truth, including in history.

The politization of America has now seeped over into the field of American history as evident by not only *The 1619 Project*, but also *Searching for Black Confederates*, which have represented the current trend of the rewriting of American history to meet and support popular political agendas of so-called "Progressivism" and the political Left. In striking contrast, this current book and my 2018 book, *Blacks in Gray Uniforms*, has been written to correct the falsifying of authentic American and Black history and the distorting of historical facts, because of today's politically corrupt and morally diseased environment that has unfortunately become so popular and fashionable as to somehow have allowed the publication of works not sufficiently grounded in historical facts, but primarily in extreme political agendas of the liberal and corrupt Left in America.

But given all of the ample evidence from both primary and secondary historical documentation, what cannot be denied was the reality and historical fact that thousands of Black Confederates who fought for the South were not only motivated to gain equality and freedom, but also to defend the Southern land where they had been born in part because the rise of Southern nationalism, when the South was invaded by Union armies. This, of course, included the forgotten Black Confederates of the full infantry battalion that had been organized in Richmond in early 1865 and which fought with distinction at the Battle of Painesville on the spring morning of April 5, 1865.

Bibliography

"Arming the Enslaved? March 13, 1865," National Park Service, Richmond National Battlefield Park, Virginia.

Brown, Christopher Leslie and Morgan, Philip D., *Arming Slaves, From Classical Times to the Modern Age*, (New Haven: Yale University Press, 2006).

Calkins, Chris M., *The Appomattox Campaign, March 29-April 9, 1865*, (Lynchburg: Schroeder Publications, 2008).

Daily Dispatch, Richmond, Virginia.

Evening Star, Washington, D.C.

Grant, Ulysses S. Grant, *Personal Memoirs of U.S. Grant*, vol. 2, (New York: Charles L. Webster and Company, 1886)

Horn, John, *The Petersburg Campaign June 1864-April 1865,* (Conshohocken: Combined Publishing, 2000).

"Hugh Hartshorne Janeway, (1842-1865)-Memorials, Find a Grave, internet.

Lanning, Michael L., *The African American Soldier: A Two Hundred Year History of African Americans in the U.S. Military,* (New York: Citadel, 2022).

Levin, Kevin M., Personal Blog, October 31, 2020.

Lloyd, William Penn, *History of the First Regiment Pennsylvania Reserve Cavalry*, (Philadelphia; King and Baird Printers, 1864).

Longacre, Edward G., *The Cavalry at Appomattox, A Tactical Study of Mounted Operations during the Civil War's Climactic Campaign, March 27-April 9, 1865*, (Mechanicsburg: Stackpole Books, 2003).

Morning Leader, Cleveland, Ohio.

New York Herald, New York, New York.

New York Times, New York, New York.

Official Report of the 1st New Jersey Cavalry Regiment, Major Walter R. Robbins, May 25, 1865, internet.

Pyne Henry R., *The History of the First New Jersey Cavalry*, (Trenton: J. A. Beecher Publisher, 1871).

Richmond Dispatch, Richmond, Virginia.

Richmond Examiner, Richmond, Virginia.

Sentinel, Richmond, Virginia.

Tucker, Phillip Thomas, *Blacks in Gray Uniforms, A New Look at the South's Most Forgotten Combat Troops 1861-1865*, (London: Fonthill Media, 2018).

Tucker, Phillip Thomas, *Brothers in Liberty, The Forgotten Story of the Free Black Haitians Who Fought for American Independence*, (Essex, Stackpole Books, 2023)

Wall Street Journal, New York, New York.

Walvin, James, *Freedom, The Overthrowing of the Slave Empires*, (New York: Pegasus Books, 2019).

Warren, Wendy, *New England Bound, Slavery and Colonization in Early America*, (New York: Liveright Publishing, 2017).

About the Author

VISIT HIS AUTHOR PAGE ON AMAZON
PHILLIP THOMAS TUCKER

OR VISIT THE AUTHOR'S WEBSITE
https://www.phillipthomastuckerphd.com/

PHILLIP THOMAS TUCKER, Ph.D., has won recognition as a national award-winning historian and America's most prolific groundbreaking "New Look" historian in multiple fields of history. He has authored more than 120 books in many fields of history, while gaining an international reputation as "the Stephen King of History." Best known for presenting fresh perspectives and original ideas to demythologize traditional history long outdated, Tucker has authored more than 190 works, both scholarly books and articles, of history that have long overturned outdated books of traditional history.

The winner of prestigious national awards and well-known as "a creative, innovative thinker, who has a gift for conceiving and outlining original works in serious history," he has emerged as America's most iconoclastic and prolific historian in the 21st Century. Tucker's groundbreaking history books have been widely praised on both sides of the Atlantic from the *New York Times* to the *London Times*. A fellow Ph.D. in history and professional historian emphasized how "Tucker is one of the most innovative, hardest working, and diligently productive" historians in America.

Tucker has become one of America's top historians in the field of Revolutionary War history, authoring groundbreaking books like GEORGE WASHINGTON'S SURPRISE ATTACK; BROTHERS OF LIBERTY; SAVING WASHINGTON'S ARMY; ALEXANDER HAMILTON'S REVOLUTION; HOW THE IRISH WON THE AMERICAN REVOLUTION; KINGS MOUNTAIN; ALEXANDER HAMITON AND THE BATTLE OF YORKTOWN; and others.

Presenting vibrant historical narratives and cutting-edge history distinguished by new perspectives and insights, the author has written more than 110 highly original books of unique distinction. Tucker's RANGER RAID has presented a close look at the most audacious and daring raid in the annals of American military history—the attack of Major Robert Rogers and his Rangers on St. Francis, while breaking much new ground in the field. This 2021 book has broadened the author's range of important books that have focused on fascinating subjects from the French and Indian War to the Second World War.

He also has completed books of international interest in the field of Women's history, including MULAN AND THE MODERN CONTROVERSY, THE UNCONQUERABLE SPIRIT OF A YOUNG AND COURAGEOUS CHINESE WOMAN; THE TRUNG SISTERS; Four Volume of the HARRIETT TUBMAN SERIES; LAKSHMI BAI; SOLITUDE OF GUADELOUPE; GRAN TOYA (Volume I of a four-volume HAITIAN REVOLUTIONARY WOMEN

SERIES), etc. He has also authored groundbreaking works in Women's history, with JOSEPHINE BAKER; MARY EDMONIA LEWIS; FEMALE APACHE WARRIOR AND SHAMAN OF HER PEOPLE, LITTLE SISTER LOZEN; CAVALRY CAPTAIN NADEZHDA DUROVA; CHARLOTTE L. FORTEN'S BROKEN HEART; OLYMPE DE GOUGES, etc.

More than 25 of Tucker's books have been written about the distinguished legacies of black heroes and heroines, including a new book about the forgotten mother of the Civil Rights Movement, CLAUDETTE COLVIN; four volumes devoted to heroine Harriet Tubman; four books about the remarkable life of female Buffalo Soldier CATHY WILLIAMS; four volumes devoted to the most famous black regiment (the 54th Massachusetts) of the Civil War; etc. He has written more than a dozen books about unforgettable black women to reveal their rich contributions and sacrifice in America's story and Caribbean history.

Very few historians have so expertly combined academic and popular history to vividly recreate the past from mere scraps of historical evidence to continuously break new ground and present fresh perspectives, while shattering historical myths and providing distinctive "New Look" perspectives to illuminate historical narratives than Tucker. Unlike traditionally told historical narratives from only one side or perspective, the author has allowed readers to view the most ignored and forgotten side of history, especially black history and women's history, to bestow a more balanced and honest perspective to the historical record.

First and foremost, Tucker's books are stores about people of all races and classes who were caught in monumental historical events beyond their control and power to escape, while presenting hard-hitting and brutally realistic and honest narratives. As much as possible, the author tells these stores through the eyes and experiences of the participants.

One of the author's most recent books has been devoted to the incredible saga of teenage Claudette Colvin, which is a heroic story of defiance and protest in the face of impossible odds. Tucker's CLAUDETTE COLVIN, FORGOTTEN MOTHER OF THE CIVIL RIGHTS MOVEMENT is an especially timely and important work for all Americans today. Significantly, Dr. Tucker has been the most prolific and groundbreaking author in black history in the last 50 years, including the books CUSTER'S FORGOTTEN BLACK SOULMATE, NAT TURNER'S HOLY WAR AGAINST SLAVERY, FATHER OF THE TUSKEGEE AIRMEN, JOHN C. ROBINSON, DAVID FAGEN (2 volumes); CHARLOTTE L. FORTEN'S BROKEN HEART; JOSEPHINE BAKER; MARY EDMONIA LEWIS, and four volumes about female Buffalo Soldier CATHY WILLIAMS.

Dr. Tucker's books are distinguished by a unique fusion of enlightenment with groundbreaking history and fresh perspectives to reveal important historical narratives that have been long-ignored and forgotten in the traditional narrative. Tucker earned national recognition in winning one of America's most prestigious national awards for the best non-fiction book in Southern history in 1993. Dr. Tucker also enjoyed a distinguished career as a Department of Defense historian, primarily in Washington, D.C., for more than two decades, including duty in working on the personal staff of the Chief of the United Sates Air Force at the Pentagon, Washington, D.C.

This prolific author has been long known for innovative and creative thinking outside the box to present different and fresh views to solve historical mysteries and overturn traditional historical viewpoints. Tucker's iconoclastic books are widely-known to be as hard-hitting as they are groundbreaking, including CUSTER AT GETTYSBURG,

A NEW LOOK AT GEORGE ARMSTRONG CUSTER VERSUS JEB STUART IN THE BATTLE'S CLIMACTIC CAVALRY CHARGES: the most important Civil War book of corrective Gettysburg history released in the 21st Century. The History Book Club lavishly praised this groundbreaking book—"a book combining two popular subjects [and] author and historian Phillip Thomas Tucker recounts the story of Custer at Gettysburg with verve."

Dr. Tucker's books have been featured by the History Book Club for more than three decades. He has earned the rare distinction as the only historian in the long history of the History Book Club whose important books have been featured for three consecutive decades.

Fellow professional historians have long recognized Dr. Tucker's "gift for conceiving and outlining original works in serious history [which is] his longest suit as a professional historian," in the words of one distinguished academic historian and fellow Ph.D. in the field of history. Even more, America's most prolific author in history in the twenty-first century has achieved recognition at "the most innovative, hardest working, and diligently productive [historian] of his generation."

Tucker's well-researched, scholarly books have presented cutting edge "New Look" history that have provided fresh views about the nation's most important turning point moments in American history. A 2020 History Book Club and Military Book Club Selection like six of the author's other books, Tucker's CUSTER AT GETTYSBURG has been acclaimed by leading experts as thoughtfully penetrating, while illuminating the most forgotten chapter of Gettysburg history. This groundbreaking book has overturned the outdated obsolete books by emphasizing the importance of the crucial cavalry role at Gettysburg on July 3, 1863. Representing the author's 7th Gettysburg book in his well-known myth busting tradition, CUSTER AT GETTYSBURG has presented a corrective analysis to explain the most neglected reason for decisive Union victory at Gettysburg, when Custer and his Michigan men saved the day.

CUSTER AT GETTYSBURG, the most scholarly book ever written about this forgotten turning point in Civil War and American history, has overturned generations of outdated Gettysburg historiography, while once again revealing the author's long-time and well-known penchant for writing groundbreaking history. The History Book Club editor wrote how this important book tells the story "Where the legend of Custer was born," and how "Custer's true rise to prominence began on the battlefield of Gettysburg [and Tucker] shows how the Custer legend was born [in] the war's most famous battle, an eye-opening new perspective on Gettysburg's overlooked cavalry battle" to reconfirm the author's widespread reputation as America's leading "New Look" historian.

By presenting cutting edge history, Dr. Tucker's many books have turned traditional historical narrative upside down to present fresh views and perspectives from meticulous research, while rewriting the romanticized, obsolete history that has been incorrectly presented to us by old school traditionalists. In consequence, Tucker has emerged as America's most groundbreaking and prolific historian, presenting corrective history of importance in a flood of groundbreaking books. This award-winning writer has written more than 5 million words in more than 100 books of unique distinction in a wide range of highly-specialized fields of history, while maintaining a high quality output of corrective history over a lengthy period of time during two different centuries: an accomplishment not achieved by any American historian during the last half century.

For decades, Dr. Tucker has bestowed recognition to forgotten women, black and white, of distinction and other ignored players in America's story to leave a lasting literary achievement in multiple fields of history. No American historian has broken more new ground in so many books of historical significance in so many diverse fields of history than this prolific author. While chronicling important lives in colorful narratives that are educational, Tucker has written uniquely human and cutting-edge history in truly iconoclastic books that enlighten and inspire readers.

The author earned a Ph.D. in American History at a prestigious Jesuit institution, St. Louis University, where he was "part of a tradition of academic excellence." Tucker then served his country for more than two decades at military bases across the United States as a Department of Defense civilian historian, including working at the Pentagon in Washington, D.C.

As noted, Tucker has often illuminated major turning point moments in American history, including his highly acclaimed PICKETT'S CHARGE, A NEW LOOK AT GETTYSBURG'S FINAL ATTACK (distributed by Simon and Schuster). This groundbreaking book was lavishly praised by Yale graduate Thomas E. Ricks, one of America's most distinguished historians, in his NEW YORK TIMES REVIEW (11/10/2016), "Thomas Ricks on the Season's Military History." Please see this NEW YORK TIMES review at:

https://www.nytimes.com/2016/11/13/books/review/new-military-history-books.html

Gettysburg expert and scholar, Bradley M. Gottfried, Ph.D., former College of Southern Maryland president, emphasized how Tucker's PICKETT'S CHARGE is "easily the best book on the topic."

The author's CUSTER AT GETTYSBURG has set the historical record straight after more than a century and a half, while revealing a forgotten turning point moment in American history: George Armstrong Custer's vital role in helping to win the Battle of Gettysburg on July 3, 1863. CUSTER AT GETTYSBURG is even a more groundbreaking and important work than Tucker's PICKETT'S CHARGE. This scholarly work has overturned the many outdated Gettysburg books by traditional authors still clinging to outdated orthodoxy and tradition. Tucker has completed another important Custer book entitled, WHY CUSTER WAS NEVER WARNED to reveal the forgotten true story about the Battle of the Little Bighorn and much like his groundbreaking DEATH AT THE LITTLE BIGHORN.

During the past decades, no historian today has broken more new ground in the Gettysburg field than Dr. Tucker, including his recent AMERICA'S BLOODY HILL OF DESTINY. Dr. Tucker has authored seven unique and important Gettysburg books with "New Look" perspectives and a distinctive Cattonesque narrative style and energetic style of writing, while providing a wealth of new ideas, fresh views, and insightful perspectives. He has overturned generations of conventional wisdom and outdated Gettysburg history in groundbreaking books like BARKSDALE'S CHARGE, THE IRISH AT GETTYSBURG, STORMING LITTLE ROUND TOP, GETTYSBURG'S MOST HELLISH BATTLEGROUND, etc.

Tucker has become the most prolific "New Look" scholar in Gettysburg, blacks, Irish, and women's studies in the 21st Century. He has presented many unique aspects of history—military, social, political, racial—in a new and fresh way, including his recent books of the new Harriet Tubman Series of four volumes. As mentioned, Tucker's books have been of an extremely groundbreaking nature never before achieved by a single author. For instance, one expert emphasized about the author's DEATH AT THE LITTLE BIGHORN how: "no one has made a stronger case for what really happened than Phillip Thomas Tucker in this compelling and convincing narration."

Even more, the author's books are distinguished by a vivid, lively descriptive style of writing unlike the dry, textbook style so common in history books. Tucker has long focused on some of America's best human interest stories and historical vignettes. Describing characters and events in great detail, the author's unique narrative style, often poetic, in overall vivid descriptiveness, has allowed readers to be transported back in time to stirring moments in history. By bringing forgotten men and women vividly back to life, Tucker has written dozens and dozens books of rare distinction that are extremely enlightening and educational. A narrative and descriptive historian with a Ph.D. who has successfully merged these dual strengths in a rare combination not often seen in any writer, Tucker has allowed readers to gain an intimate feel for history like few other authors today. Most important, Dr. Tucker has become America's most prolific ground-breaking historian in many fields of history: an unprecedented achievement to date.

An innovative, out-of-the-box thinker recognized on both sides of the Atlantic, Tucker has authored highly original "New Look" narratives to reveal new insights and perspectives to prove that the best history definitely goes against the grain and tradition. Insightful and thoughtful Daniel N. White emphasized a fundamental truth in his 9/20/2011 review of the author's myth-busting EXODUS FROM THE ALAMO: "Finally, The Truth About the Alamo."

Tucker earned three history degrees from prestigious universities, including a Ph.D. in American history from St. Louis University in 1990, while gaining a 4.00 GPA. In books distinguished by their broad human appeal and fresh interpretations, the author has most often untangled historical half-truths to present more accurate history by more deeply exploring the deep complexities of the human experience on multiple levels, such as the lives of Buffalo Soldiers David Fagen and Cathy Williams.

Significantly, this myth-busting historian has also illuminated some of the most climactic and crescendo moments in American history from the American Revolution to the Second World War, while establishing new literary benchmarks in Women's, African American, Caribbean, American Revolutionary War, Tuskegee, Civil War, Abolition, Buffalo Soldier, Irish, Little Bighorn, Pirate, Aviation, Western, Spanish-American War, Gettysburg, and Southern history.

As noted, Tucker's iconoclastic books have especially bestowed greater recognition to long-ignored African American men and women. The author has emerged as one of the most important historians in the field of African American history like in other fields of history in the last century. The author's groundbreaking series (54th MASSACHUSETTS GLORY SERIES of four volumes) of books have celebrated the heroics of the North's first black regiment during the Civil War: the first series of books ever devoted to this remarkable black regiment that brought forth a new birth of freedom to America.

Significantly, Dr. Tucker's books about black history have also focused on bringing about greater social awareness to Americans, both black and white, today, about black heroes and heroines who have been long overlooked and forgotten. In highly original "New Look" narratives, the author has promoted the heroics of brave African American men, aviator pioneer John C. Robinson, and black women from the American Revolution to the Second World War, including multiple series of important and groundbreaking books.

As noted, Tucker's "New Look" books have focused on the heavily Buffalo Soldier experience (2 volumes about David Fagen and 4 volumes about Harriet Tubman) and

Jamaica's national heroine Nanny and revolutionary women of Haiti. Tucker's first book (2002) about the remarkable life of female Buffalo Soldier Cathy Williams was praised by Library Journal: "A unique story of gender and race . . . that reaches across categories, from American, African American, and military history to Western and Women's history."

Like his other revealing books in African American history, Tucker has accomplished a comparable significant literary feat in the fascinating field of Irish history like in black history. The author has written about the forgotten Irish contributions in the Civil War, Texas Revolution, and westward expansion, including: HOW THE IRISH WON THE AMERICAN REVOLUTION; THE IRISH AT GETTYSBURG; GOD HELP THE IRISH! HISTORY OF THE IRISH BRIGADE, and other noteworthy books, including award winners.

Talented historian and scholar Perry D. Jamieson, Ph.D., emphasized how: "What separates [Tucker] from many other historians is that he is an innovative 'idea person.' I have known very few historians who can match his ability to conceive a topic, develop a fresh approach to it, and write about it at length."

In correcting the historical record in his national award-winners, Best Sellers, and History and Military Book Club Main Selections, Tucker has overturned America's oldest prevailing myths and stereotypes, especially racial, in multiple fields of history. From the beginning, a historian's greatest gift has been to present the familiar in new ways and this achievement has become Dr. Tucker's expertise and specialty.

Most of all, Tucker's books have reinterpreted history around the world to provide a good many fresh and new perspectives, allowing a new generation of readers to rediscover America's fascinating past through a sharper lens and more intensified focus, especially in terms of race and gender. One professor emphasized Tucker's educational contributions that have brought history alive like few other historians: "thousands of tourists may now be exposed to what has been washed out by narratives" for generations.

By conceiving original history in multiple fields, he has emerged today as America's leading corrective historian and deconstructionist of outdated history. Described as a "once in a generation historian," Tucker has authored ground-breaking "New Look" books that present unique perspectives for the twenty-first century, while overturning the traditional historical narrative. One revered historian concluded: "Dr. Tucker is one of the two or three best 'idea persons' that I've met during my nearly twenty years as a professional military historian." By digging deeper to solve history's mysteries and to unravel its many riddles, Tucker has dismantled some of the most sacred cows in American history.

Throughout his long career, Dr. Tucker has always taken the road least traveled by historians by focusing on unique "New Look" perspectives in vivid historical narratives that have been groundbreaking. Tucker has praised the American fighting man, while simultaneously promoting greater social awareness. Struggles against the odds and convention by forgotten underdog players have been a primary theme of Tucker's many biographies, especially those about African American women. One professor praised this award-winning author educated at St. Louis University "for making the study of mankind a real narrative."

The author's many books are distinguished by their overall humanity to reveal history's most intimate and personal side, which has been too often ignored by other historians. In one astute reviewer's words: "Most history in printed form has very little, if any humanity [but the author's books] made a profound impact on me, due not only to razor-sharp depictions of strategy and its execution, but something that was revealed with astonishing empathy: the Truth."

Tucker's books have most often gone against the grain of the traditional consensus and standard narrative to present some of the most fascinating chapters of America's most hidden history by focusing on revealing long-silenced voices and stories long forgotten. One historian emphasized that in Tucker's DEATH AT THE LITTLE BIGHORN: "Custer's Last movements and decisions have been argued about since 1876, but, in my mind, no one has made a stronger case for what really happened than Phillip Thomas Tucker in this compelling and convincing narration."

PICKETT'S CHARGE (Main Selection of the History Book Club) also garnered considerable praise from leading experts across America. One reviewer emphasized how the author "Replaces 150 years of uninterrogated mythology with meticulously research history to give us a new and long-overdue understanding" of this key turning point moment in American history.

Tucker's "New Look" 2010 EXODUS FROM THE ALAMO, THE ANATOMY OF THE LAST STAND MYTH (a History Book Club Selection sold at the Alamo for years and to this day) has overturned generations of mythical Texas history, which has been grossly distorted for nearly two centuries. A *Library Journal* review emphasized that "Tucker provides long-overdue corrections to the Alamo story unknown to most readers." Another reviewer concluded: "I commend Phillip Thomas Tucker for uncovering the ugly truth" about Texas and its dark history, especially when it came to slavery and race relations. In mid-August 2011, *The Times* and *Daily Mail* of London, England, featured complimentary lead stories that praised "Exodus from the Alamo."

FAKE AMAZON 1-Star and 2-Star ATTACK REVIEWS: One contributor to a Civil War blog revealed the motivation behind an organized campaign of rivals who have engaged in years of posting fake 1-star Amazon reviews for the author's books in an organized smear campaign: "Did you pan it on Amazon? . . . stop Tucker before he writes again." Only one or two cyber cowards (false and fake attack reviews that are excessively editor obsessive since they obviously came from a rival editor and publisher) have been behind the posting of more than 250 fake 1-star Amazon reviews against the author's works for more than a decade. One publisher, whose editors of Tucker's books have been repeatedly smeared by them with their lies, concluded how "they are simply scum."

EXODUS FROM THE ALAMO Reviews by Leading Experts:
—"The research is hard to argue against [and] is pretty straight forward. Read all of it with an open mind [and] You will surprise yourself," *Kepler's Military History.*
—"Tucker provides long-overdue corrections to the Alamo story unknown to most readers," *Library Journal.*
—"Tucker has written a remarkable account of one of America's pivotal military actions," *Military Heritage Magazine.*
—"Tucker's bold assessment is undeniably true," *City Book Review.*
—"My, My, My, we now have a truthful book about the Alamo [by the] complete demolition of the Texas founding myth done here," Dandelion Salad Review "Finally, The Truth About the Alamo," by Daniel N. White, Sept. 20, 2011.
—"An eye-opening reappraisal of what really happened [at] the Alamo [and] Tucker's well researched account dramatically rewrites long-accepted history and shatters

some of the most cherished and enduring myths of the 1836 battle," *Armchair General*.

—"Readers open to new interpretations . . . will find compelling arguments within its well-researched pages," *Dallas Morning Star*.

—"It is refreshing for historians to challenge the conventions of history," Army Magazine.

In reviewer Daniel N. White's words: "The elephant in Texas history's living room has always been . . . slavery," and Tucker has exposed this fact in full.

In his complimentary NEW YORK TIMES review (Nov. 10, 2016), Thomas E. Ricks praised PICKETT'S CHARGE: "Tucker, who has written many books of military history, makes the contrarian argument [but] the book is most interesting for the bright nuggets of information Tucker presents . . . a mosaic of thousands of pieces that, seen whole, amounts to a fascinating picture of what was probably the most important moment of the Civil War [with] new facts, different perspectives."

Indeed, most of all, Tucker's "New Look" books have provided a great many fresh insights about America's most defining and climactic turning moments of the nation's story. He has most often illuminated historical blind spots, while correcting "old school" narratives of America's most iconic moments. Even more, he has employed a host of new ways of presenting historical evidence to provide fresh interpretations and analysis of a groundbreaking nature. Quite simply, decade after decade, Dr. Tucker has never written "your father's history" and never will. One professor emphasized Tucker's long-time role in shattering myths in multiple fields of history: "it is so good to know that we have academic warriors."

The author's first-ever and award-winning biographies of men and women of all races and creeds have brilliantly illuminated the forgotten lives of underdogs, lost souls, rebels, outcasts, renegades, deserters, generals, Buffalo Soldiers, Tuskegee Airmen, pirates, misfits, nonconformists, and refugees, while going against the grain to reveal long-overlooked historical truths, forgotten narratives, and hidden history.

For example, Tucker has also presented an "unvarnished look" in his "ground-breaking new analysis at one of America's iconic battles" to completely overturn the long-entrenched traditional views, myths, and stereotypes, which have been falsely created. Consequently, EXODUS FROM THE ALAMO garnered "an exemplary series of reviews from objective publications and scholars" on both sides of the Atlantic.

In demystifying America's iconic turning point moments, Tucker's unique "New Look" perspectives of his books have allowed readers to rethink history and the overall human experience in an entirely new way. He has illuminated history in an entirely new light and from fresh perspectives to expose long-existing misconceptions and entrench myths.

The author's unique penchant for presenting unvarnished historical truths through an unfiltered lens has repeatedly overturned traditional history and generations of conventional thought, while revealing the truth about "taboo" perspectives long avoided by other historians. The author's groundbreaking books bring to life forgotten men and women long banished to history's most obscure margins, while bestowing credit and recognition where it is rightfully due.

AMERICA'S TOP ACADEMICS LAVISHLY PRAISE "NEW LOOK" BOOKS:

Tucker's PICKETT'S CHARGE has presented many fresh views and new perspectives to overturn generations of stale and obsolete Gettysburg history. This "magisterial" book about a turning point moment in American history during the most decisive battle of the Civil War has been highly-praised by America's top academics and leading Civil War and Gettysburg historians.

The *New York Times* review of PICKETT'S CHARGE praised the author's original and fresh approach:
—Tucker's "Pickett's Charge, A New Look at Gettysburg's Final Attack offers a vastly (and intriguingly) different spin on your average assessment of the presumed futility of the attack." *HistoryNet.*
—Historian Alan Axelrod, Ph.D.: "Phillip Thomas Tucker's magisterial Pickett's Charge: A New Look at Gettysburg's finally replaces 150-plus years of uninterrogated mythology with meticulously researched history to give us a new and long-overdue understanding."
—William C. Davis emphasized: "In his almost minute-by-minute account of the most famous infantry charge in history, Phillip Thomas Tucker provides a thoughtful and challenging new look at the great assault at Gettysburg, from planning to aftermath. Not afraid to lay blame where he thinks it belongs, Tucker is fresh and bold in his analysis and use of sources."
—Louis P. Masur, Distinguished Professor of American Studies and History, Rutgers University: "A thought-provoking and eye-opening study of this pivotal moment in American history."
—"the author does a workman-like job of revising many myths and misconceptions about the battle [and] takes issue with many of the long-held assumptions and analysis of the famous attack and seeks to revise many long-held misconceptions" Jerry D. Lenaburg, Graduate of the United States Naval Academy and Senior DoD Military Analyst, *New York Journal of Books.*
—"A popular historian deconstructs 'the greatest assault of the greatest battle of America's greatest war'," *Kirkus Reviews.*

—"No action in the Civil War is more iconic than the misnamed 'Pickett's Charge,' and yet few episodes of this most studied of wars is in need of more enlightened and enlightening reexamination [until] Phillip Thomas Tucker's magisterial Pickett's Charge," Alan Axelrod, Ph.D.

—"Pickett's Charge, A New Look at Gettysburg's Final Attack is a detailed analysis of one of the most iconic and defining moments in American history. This book presents a much-needed fresh look, including the unvarnished truths and ugly realities about the

unforgettable story," Press Release.

—"Tucker officers a fresh account of Gettysburg's final attack [and] reveals the tactical brilliance of a master plan that went awry. Drawing on ample primary sources . . . Pickett's Charge details the complexities and contradictions of one of the pivotal moments in our nation's defining contests." History Book Club and Military Book Club

—"Phillip Thomas Tucker's new book 'Pickett's Charge' . . . reveals the incredible Irish underpinnings of the day that changed America forever . . . Tucker sets out to quash two myths that have fueled Civil War debate for 150 years [and] The first of these is that Pickett's Charge was an ill-advised roll of the dice [and] The second myth is that Pickett's Charge, like the broader Confederate war effort, was Anglo-Saxon in its leadership and execution . . . Tucker introduces us to the Irish-born and the sons of the Irish-born" men of Pickett's Charge and "Tucker has restored a vital part of our history in America." *IrishCentral.*

DEATH AT THE LITTLE BIGHORN was still another History Book Club and Military Book Club selection like PICKETT's CHARGE and numerous other books by Dr. Tucker, including his recent ALEXANDER HAMILTON AND THE BATTLE OF YORKTOWN 1781 in 2022. These ground-breaking books have garnered praise for presenting a good many fresh perspectives and new views that have overturned the standard interpretations of generations of historians. In regard to Tucker's DEATH AT THE LITTLE BIGHORN:

—"Custer's last movements and decisions have been argued about since 1876, but, in my mind, no one has made a stronger case for what really happened [at the Little Bighorn] than Phillip Thomas Tucker," Robert Boze Bell, Executive Editor of *True West Magazine*, about Tucker's book.

—"Presents a fascinating, lively, and important reassessment of the famous Battle of the Little Bighorn . . . Where the 'Last Stand' happened and what it means will change dramatically for readers of this book." Clyde A. Milner, II, co-editor of *The Oxford History of the American West*.

—"Phillip Thomas Tucker [emphasized] that the true turning point of the battle came early with the charge at Medicine Tail Coulee Ford." *Wild West Magazine*.

ADDITIONAL ACCLAIM FROM LEADING EXPERTS:

Premier historian James M. McPherson, Ph.D., winner of the Pulitzer Prize and the George Henry Davis '86 Professor Emeritus of United States History at Princeton University, wrote how Tucker is "one of the most prolific Civil War historians" in America. Tucker's "PICKETT'S CHARGE" has continued his ground-breaking Gettysburg scholarship distinguished by new and original perspectives in groundbreaking words. The author's groundbreaking STORMING LITTLE ROUND TOP was described as "extremely well-researched and well-written," Choice.

Tucker's groundbreaking PICKETT'S and DEATH AT THE LITTLE BIGHORN (both History Book Club Selections) are "New Look" books that have presented a more inclusive approach, providing readers with a thorough and deep understanding of these pivotal moments in American history.

Talented historian Allen Carl Guelzo has also praised the author's books: "Phillip Thomas Tucker, who has written on topics as varied as the Alamo, the Revolutionary War, and African American soldiers [has produced a] narrative [that] is thickly sprinkled with commentary from diaries and letters."

In regard to Dr. Tucker's highly acclaimed BARKSDALE'S CHARGE at Gettysburg, Jerry D. Morelock, Ph.D., emphasized how, "The author of the acclaimed Exodus from the Alamo does more 'myth busting' in this superbly argued book."

—Terrence Winchell, National Park Service Historian, emphasized how "Tucker has produced a wonderful addition to the library of the most discerning Gettysburg collector."

—Scholar Darryl E. Brock, Ph.D., also praised PICKETT'S CHARGE: "Presenting an exhilarating narrative based on rigorous re-interpretation of historical sources, scholars and lay readers alike soon recognize the Southern nation's high watermark as the second day at Gettysburg." In still another milestone study of a groundbreaking nature, Tucker's PICKETT'S CHARGE has continued his tradition of presenting "New Look" perspectives to correct stale Gettysburg historiography.

—Dr. Edward G. Longacre emphasized how "Burnside's Bridge highlights a significant but neglected aspect of Antietam [and] the author's scholarship is sound, his grasp of tactics sure, and his writing vivid, making Burnside's Bridge both a good read and good history."

—Likewise, the *Journal of Southern History* praised BURNSIDE'S BRIDGE: "Tucker offers a blow-by-blow account of the fight for the lower Antietam . . . Tucker deserves considerable praise for his efforts. Drawing upon a truly impressive range of primary and secondary sources, he has produced a thorough and highly readable narrative."

—William C. Davis, one of America's leading historians, wrote: "'The Thermopylae of the Civil War' . . . the single most remembered aspect of the fight, the contest for the bridge, has not until now been the subject of an in-depth book-length study. Phillip Thomas Tucker remedies this in *Burnside's Bridge* . . . In a work thoroughly researched and dramatically written, Tucker lays out the story" in dramatic fashion.

From BURNSIDE'S BRIDGE to PICKETT'S CHARGE that focused on the crucial eastern theater and to equally ground-breaking books about the western theater, Tucker has most often emphasized the most ignored and forgotten aspects of the Civil War. Tucker's books have illuminated the American experience to present multi-dimensional perspectives combined with groundbreaking narratives. Utilizing a rare ability to demythologize history regardless of the nation and century, Tucker has most often reinterpreted the outdated historical record and the most iconic moments of American history, while breathing new life into the outdated traditional narratives.

Dr. Tucker has long focused on exploring the most hidden history to expose misconceptions and correct the historical record long in need of fresh and new analysis for the 21st century. Tucker has presented the good, bad, and ugly of history by relying on primary documentation mined from little-known private and public collections, especially from Mexico, in his groundbreaking EXODUS FROM THE ALAMO. Tucker's EXODUS FROM THE ALAMO has also won widespread acclaim:

—"The research is hard to argue against [and] is pretty straight forward. Read all of it with an open mind before drawing your own conclusions. You just might surprise yourself." *Kepler's Military History.*

—"Exodus from the Alamo offers a fresh and fascinating look at [the Alamo and] Tucker's efforts to include all pertinent evidence, including that of previously ignored Mexican sources, pays off in the form of a relevant and thoroughly researched book."

—"A necessary read for anyone interested in the Texas war of Independence." *Strategy Page.*

—"demonstrating a mastery and understanding" of the Alamo's mysteries. *Journal of America's Military Past.*

—"Dr. Tucker examines the real story behind the premier symbol of Texas . . . courageous as it is insightful, Exodus from the Alamo is a major contribution . . ." Antonio Zavaleta, Ph.D.

"I've just finished reading an extraordinary book, Exodus from the Alamo [from] reliable overlooked sources." *Present Progressive.*

Tucker has most often unearthed a good many long-overlooked aspects of ethnic and social history to significantly fill the wide cultural and social gaps in the narratives of America's story. Rewriting America's most iconic moments in great detail by relying on new sources of information, Dr. Tucker has brought vividly to life fascinating personalities in first-ever biographies about America's female Buffalo Soldier CATHY WILLIAMS (4 volumes); EMILY D. WEST; DAVID FAGEN (2 volumes); JOHN C. ROGINSON, FATHER OF THE TUSKEGEE AIRMEN; and four remarkable women of the HAITIAN REVOLUTIONARY WOMEN SERIES. Most important, all of these books have gained widespread praise.

—Professor Mario Marcel Salas, University of Texas, wrote: "Tucker knows how to mine the data for details lying well below the surface and use them to create an exhilarating narrative. This book demonstrates the power of analysis and the ability of the author to tell of the African American experience."

—Professor Tim Carmichael: "This engaging biography of John C. Robinson, the 'Brown Condor,' gives the aviation pioneer his historical due and . . . makes an important contribution to our knowledge."

— Edward G. Longacre, Ph.D.: *"Brothers in Liberty* recounts the long-neglected, historically and culturally important story of the free Blacks and mulattoes of Saint-Domingue (modern-day Haiti) in aid of American and French forces during the October 1779 battle of Savannah. The critical role played by the Chasseurs Volontaires in helping reverse the fortunes of the disastrous offensive against the British-held city has never been chronicled in such detail and with such deep feeling for the larger-than-military issues involved. Here is another characteristic effort by the Stephen King of American history."

Over a period of decades, Dr. Tucker has evolved into "the most innovative, hardest working, and diligently productive historian of his generation," in the words of one historian, for having authored more than 110 books of groundbreaking history. These books have brought many forgotten personalities vividly to life to illuminate the histories of many nations around the world by exploring remarkable lives.

Printed in Great Britain
by Amazon